MY LIFE, MY FIGHT
STEVEN ADAMS

MY LIFE, MY FIGHT

RISING UP FROM NEW ZEALAND
TO THE OKC THUNDER

STEVEN ADAMS

with **MADELEINE CHAPMAN**

hachette
BOOKS

NEW YORK   BOSTON

Hachette Books
Hachette Book Group
1290 Avenue of the Americas
New York, NY 10104
HachetteBookGroup.com

First published by Penguin Random House New Zealand in 2018

The moral right of Madeleine Chapman to be identified as the author has been asserted.

First U.S. Edition: October 2018

Hachette Books is a division of Hachette Book Group, Inc. The Hachette Books name and logo are trademarks of Hachette Book Group, Inc.

The publisher is not responsible for websites (or their content) that are not owned by the publisher.

The Hachette Speakers Bureau provides a wide range of authors for speaking events. To find out more, go to www.hachettespeakersbureau.com or call (866) 376-6591.

Library of Congress Control Number: 2018954174

ISBN: 978-0-316-49146-4 (hardcover); 978-0-316-49145-7 (ebook)

Printed in the United States of America

LSC-C

10 9 8 7 6 5 4 3 2 1

CONTENTS

PROLOGUE:

DRAFT NIGHT

Whatever you do, don't trip up the stairs.

I didn't care which organization drafted me. I didn't care who my future teammates would be. All I cared about was not falling over in front of the world. I repeated this to myself as the NBA commissioner, David Stern, walked on stage to loud boos from a Brooklyn crowd.

My brothers Mohi and Sid had flown over from New Zealand to be with me for the 2013 draft, and I looked across to see if they knew what was going on. They shrugged their shoulders and seemed as confused as I was. What did we know? We were just three farming brothers from Rotorua, and yet here we were on one of the biggest nights of the American sporting calendar, waiting to see which NBA team I'd be playing for next season and acting like we wore fancy suits all the time.

David Stern kept talking and the crowd kept booing. When

he congratulated the Miami Heat on winning another championship, the booing got louder. What I didn't realize was this was Stern's last draft and the crowd was using the occasion to make its feelings known about the polarizing commissioner. I scanned the crowd at the Barclays Center, which was packed with die-hard NBA fans who probably cared about basketball more than I did. I'd never been an NBA fan, I didn't even have a favorite player, and I had certainly never watched the draft before.

Above the boos, Stern could be heard announcing the first draft pick. "The first pick of the 2013 NBA draft will be made by the Cleveland Cavaliers, who have five minutes to make their selection."

Then silence. When you watch the draft at home you get to hear the ESPN analysts predicting who they think will be picked, and although they're almost always wrong at least it's something. In the arena it was completely silent while we waited for the Cavaliers to make their decision.

My brothers and I spent those five minutes staring at one of the other draft hopefuls, who was sitting with his entourage just a few tables away from us. This guy was a big star in the lead-up to the draft and was one of the favorites to be picked first. I didn't really know him. All I knew was that we were complete opposites. He seemed to have been a superstar all his life. He was a standout in high school and then played for one of the top college teams. Even though I had no real interest in college basketball outside of my own team, I knew his college was a sporting powerhouse.

Meanwhile I was a player who, as the analysts would later say, was an unknown until I declared for the draft and went to the

NBA Draft Combine testing in Chicago, where draftees are put through a series of physical tests, interviews, and scrimmages. This guy only appeared at the combine for the physical measurements, and he was still a solid bet at the number-one pick. He wasn't at any of the 12 workouts I did for 11 different teams either. He was already famous, while I was desperately working to impress anyone who had the power to hire me. But on that night, I knew exactly what was stitched on the inside of his suit jacket.

Basketball players are tall. Even the shortest are above average height. So when a bunch of basketball players are preparing for one of the biggest nights of their lives, they need a custom-tailored suit. I was sent to an agency that tailored for tall guys like me and asked what I wanted in a suit. To be honest, I just wanted it to fit. They asked what colors represented New Zealand. Damn, how should I know? They suggested green lining to represent the farmland. Sure, why not? For the tie they suggested white stripes to represent milk and dairy farming. It all seemed a bit bougie to me, but I knew nothing about fashion so I just nodded and said that sounded great. The one request I did have was for the New Zealand flag to be stitched into the lining. It wasn't an unusual request. Some players get their college logo, but I wanted to represent New Zealand through and through.

I was told to collect my suit from the agency the day before the draft. When I walked into the room, the first thing I noticed was a Cleveland Cavaliers singlet laid out with the logo cut out. One of the women told me a player had asked for the Cavaliers' logo to be sewn into the lining of his jacket. I thought that was bloody brave. No player knows for sure where they're going to end up and no organization knows for sure which player they'll pick until they do it on the night. I had an inkling that I was going to go to Oklahoma City because of the way my visits there had gone, but I would never have dared tell anyone, let alone stitch the Oklahoma City Thunder logo into the lining of my suit.

I needed to know who the man was with the biggest balls in the draft. So while I was looking through the rack for my suit, I had a peek at all the other players' outfits. All of them were pretty standard until I saw one that had a college team's singlet number on one side of the lining and on the other was the logo of the Cleveland Cavaliers. I couldn't believe this guy was that confident, and somehow I knew right then that the Cavaliers wouldn't pick him first. The universe wouldn't let anything work out that smoothly. I regretted not putting the logo of the Manawatu Jets basketball team on the other side of my jacket just for shits and giggles. It seemed as appropriate as a Cavaliers logo. When I told my brothers, we all agreed it was a bots move, then went back to worrying about my own future.

David Stern came back on stage to announce the first pick.

"With the first pick in the 2013 NBA Draft, the Cleveland Cavaliers select Anthony Bennett."

The whole room gasped. The ESPN guys yelled in surprise. This guy's table stared at the floor like someone had just died. I've never seen a group of people look so disappointed at such a joyous occasion. If the camera had cut to our table, it would have shown all of us with our mouths wide open, trying not to laugh. It was an amazing moment.

People seemed to feel sorry for him, but not me. We were all about to be recruited by an NBA team and live our dream. Not one of us deserved anyone's sympathy. We were the luckiest guys in the world that night.

When this guy was finally selected, I watched as he flashed one side of his jacket and then held the other side shut while he shook David Stern's hand on stage. There was an audible sigh of relief throughout the room when his name was read out, as if being selected in an NBA draft was some kind of torture.

The Phoenix Suns were on the clock for the fifth pick of the draft. I'd been to Phoenix for a workout and really liked it there. It was bloody hot, but I didn't mind it because it reminded me of Tonga. The Suns had seemed quite interested in me, and it was a thrill when my agent, Darren "Mats" Matsubara, got a call from them on the night.

When you watch the draft on TV, it looks like the floor of the arena is filled with the players and their support teams. But what you don't see is that the other half is packed with media and agents frantically calling organizations and sorting deals for their players. It's one of the busiest nights for them. I was glad all I had to do was sit there and not pick my nose on camera.

All players go into the draft not knowing where they'll end up, but the announcement of their name isn't a complete surprise because the managers of each team will call the player's agent five minutes before they announce their pick. Not every call to an agent ends in a contract, though. The Suns called Mats and they talked for a bit, and then they picked Alex Len, a 7'1" center from Ukraine. I have no idea what was said in that phone call and I've never asked. For all I know, they dialed the wrong number.

It was slowly dawning on me that my life was about to change. I was predicted to go somewhere between 10 and 20 in the draft, and it was getting close. But I was starving. It was a huge event and we got all dressed up and sat at tables, so I assumed they would at least feed us. But there was no food. Like, at all. The only thing on the table was a bottle of Gatorade because it's a major sponsor of the NBA. By the eighth pick I was thirsty and clammy and wanted a drink, so I grabbed the bottle and went to open it, but it was glued shut. They actually put Gatorade bottles in front of a bunch of nervous athletes and then glued them shut so we couldn't drink it.

I was starting to expect free stuff from any NBA-related events. I mean, who doesn't love free stuff? The day before I'd gone room to room at the hotel and picked up free swag bags from a bunch of big companies. They all wanted their stuff worn and used by the next batch of NBA players, but they weren't too keen on me, probably because I was dressed scruffy as. I didn't look like I was about to be recruited by anyone.

As the picks kept going—Detroit, Utah, Portland, Philadelphia— I started to lean heavily in my mind on Oklahoma City. They were my best shot with the twelfth pick. I was supposed to go in the top 15 because I was in the green room, the floor of the arena, where players get their own tables and the NBA pays for their families to be there. I wasn't exactly getting nervous, but I thought it would be mean to go to the Thunder at 12. As Michael Carter-Williams walked off stage after being selected by the Philadelphia 76ers, Mats got a phone call from the Thunder management. He talked for a minute and I fidgeted, hoping it wasn't a prank call. David Stern walked back out to announce the twelfth pick. For the first time that night I wished the crowd would stop booing so I could hear his voice crystal clear. All I could think was—if he calls your name, don't trip or stumble when you go up the stairs.

"With the twelfth pick in the 2013 NBA draft..."

Don't fall over.

"the Oklahoma City Thunder select..."

Don't stumble.

"Steven Adams."

That was it. I didn't hear the rest. I barely noticed Stern absolutely butchering the pronunciation of my hometown, Rotorua. I stood up on cue, hugged Sid, hugged Mohi, hugged my mentor and coach Kenny McFadden, hugged Mats, and high-fived his daughter. That was my team. The only other person I wish could have been there was my sister Viv, but that's another story.

Before I could move, a woman hurried over with an OKC Thunder hat and I suddenly had a whole new problem—my massive head. My dome had been measured before the event, but I still had a feeling the hat wouldn't fit, because my head is huge. When I put it on I could tell it was going to be a tight fit, so I just sat it on top of my head and left it there. I think I pulled off the look quite nicely.

Thanks to the mantra I'd been chanting in my head all night, I made it up the stairs smoothly and shook Stern's hand. Some of the earlier players had gone for a brother handshake with a hug as well, but I wasn't ready to take that risk so we shook hands like two businessmen meeting for the first time. In my mind at that point the only thing worse than tripping up the stairs would have been doing a weird, crumbly handshake-hug combo with Stern that people would mock forever.

Still not entirely sure that everything was real, I left the stage and was told I would be interviewed by Shane Battier, who had just won a championship with the Miami Heat. Everyone had said Shane was a cool guy so I tried to chat with him before our broadcast interview, but he just ignored me. I was thinking, "Man, what a dick," but then I saw he was wearing an earpiece and was probably being told all my bio information at the same time. Our interview was sweet. I got to show off the New Zealand flag in my suit and give a shout-out to everyone at home watching and cheering me on. And then it was over, and I was ushered through to the back where there was a massive press room and I had to do interviews for two hours. I remember barely any of it except that one channel had sent a little kid along to interview us. He was cute and pretty funny, but it's quite hard to hold a conversation about basketball with a five-year-old.

Some reporters wanted me to read random shout-outs, which I happily did. My dopamine levels were through the roof, and I probably would have said and done anything that anyone asked. I'm too scared to watch any interviews from that night because I swear my voice went up a full octave I was so happy. I made a video for Facebook saying thank you to everyone in New Zealand who had supported me, and for some reason I was sweating all through it, even though I hadn't done anything strenuous all day.

By the time all the interviews had wrapped up I was still on a massive high and had forgotten I hadn't eaten in hours. My agency put on a dinner for me and a couple of the other drafted players they represented. By the time we ate it was 2 a.m. and I was knocked out. I heard that some other agencies had thrown parties for their players, and I was secretly glad mine hadn't because I just wanted to eat and then pass out for 12 hours.

The next morning I woke up and didn't know what to do. After years of working towards one goal—to get to the NBA—I'd made it. Now what? I obviously knew that I'd have to move to Oklahoma and work hard in the off-season to make the roster, but what was I supposed to do the day after being drafted into the NBA?

Turns out, nothing. Everything started being done for me. The owner of the Thunder sent his private plane to New York to fly me, my family, Andre Roberson (who OKC also drafted), and his family out to Oklahoma City immediately. I posted a photo on Facebook of us in front of the plane and some people thought I'd splashed out and bought a plane already. I hadn't even been paid yet. Besides, NBA rookies get paid SUV money, not private plane money.

My brothers and I were buzzing out, trying to imagine having so much money you could afford your own plane. Once we got up in the air, it was a relief to be away from all the hype and media that had surrounded us the whole week. Some of the guys dozed off or ordered food, but all I could do was sit and try to make sense of everything. I was just a scruffy kid from Rotorua, known around town as "one of those Adams kids."

Being an NBA player hadn't been a lifelong dream of mine, it had been a six-year goal. Up to that point I was just Sid Adams's youngest boy, destined for the farm life. But here I was, being flown in a private plane to begin a dream I'd barely had time to register as being possible.

As Oklahoma City came into view and we began our descent into my new life, I wondered what my dad would have thought of all this.

1.
EVERYTHING STINKS

My hometown stinks. Literally. It stinks of rotten eggs, caused by the sulfur dioxide that rises out of the geysers, mud pools, and hot pools in the geothermally active city. When you live there you don't even notice it, but it's one of the things it's famous for. Tourists love the hot pools and the Māori culture and attractions.

Even though Rotorua is a tourist town, there's not much to do there if you are poor, which we were, especially since Dad's pension was the only income. The kindergarten that all of the Adams kids went to was just around the corner from where we lived. The primary school was just around the opposite corner. The intermediate school was next door to the primary school. And the college was one street over. Basically, I spent my childhood within walking distance of my house at all times.

Dad had lived in our house for 30 years. One day, while his two eldest were still young, Dad walked by a house that he liked the look of. It wasn't a big house or a flash one, but it was built from bricks and looked like it could handle a storm or two. The perfect house for Sid Adams. Instead of offering to buy it, he bought some land and drew up a plan to build one exactly like it for himself. I'm told that Dad was at the construction site constantly, helping the builders and making sure nobody was doing a crappy job. If Dad had one motto he lived by, it was "Whatever you do, do it well."

When the house was completed and his then small family moved in, he was living the Kiwi dream: three bedrooms on a quarter acre of land. I guess he only planned to have enough children for three bedrooms, but as his family grew and grew, so did his home. Two self-contained units were added out back behind the garage, this time with Dad doing all the work himself. Over time, when the main house got a bit crowded or one of the kids was old enough, they'd move out to one of "the baches," as they were nicknamed. It was still technically living at home but with the advantage of there being some distance from the rules of the main house.

Sid's family of kids kept growing until the morning of 23 July 1993. That's when my mum, Heilala, was taken into Rotorua Hospital for an emergency cesarean section after doctors became worried about how big her unborn baby was getting. Later that day I was born—Sid's last child.

People always ask me what it was like to grow up with so many siblings, but I spent most of my childhood with just Sid (junior), Lisa, and Gabby. Together we were the fantastic four. We were Dad's last batch of kids and by the time we were going to school most of our older siblings lived in different cities or were starting their own families. My eldest sister, Viv, who was in her thirties when I was born, lived just down the road, and as her kids are about the same age as us four, we grew up together. Technically, her kids are our nieces and nephews, but it felt weird to call them that. Unless we were fighting and trying to get the upper hand by making them call us aunty and uncle, they were just our cousins.

When I started at Owhata primary school, I joined in the morning routine with my siblings. Every morning, Dad would wake up before us, make a massive pile of toast, brew a big jug of Milo, and then sit down in his chair to watch TV and read the newspaper, which we took turns to fetch from a petrol station just across the road from our house. The petrol station workers knew Dad and us kids and sometimes gave us the paper free. Dad was so tight with his money that he gladly took the freebie even though the paper only cost a dollar. I remember he would sit at the table and drink a lot of black coffee that tasted like tar, and because I wanted to do everything that Dad did, I would drink it too. No wonder my teachers had trouble getting me to stop bouncing off the walls all day.

At school I got picked on quite a bit. I wasn't a massive kid, in fact I was quite scrawny, and I always wore the same clothes and walked around barefoot most of the time. My brother Sid, who is four years older than me, was always bigger and tougher than the other kids so if anyone tried to talk crap about him or us, he'd smash them. Gabby and Lisa were just as tall and strong and so were also good to have around as protectors. But I think most of the bullying I experienced was done by older kids who Sid used to pick on and who wanted their revenge on the Adams family.

One time, I was walking home from school and some older kids started throwing rocks at me. I didn't know what to do so I just kept walking and let them hit me. Gabby saw me and ran over and we walked home together, getting pelted by stones. When we got home, we cried to Dad, but he just looked at us like we were idiots for not throwing anything back. I thought that was the end of it until a few days later when the same kid had me up against the wall by the pool and Sid ran over and beat him up. I was enjoying the fight until he yelled at me to piss off. I realized Sid wasn't doing it because he liked me or Gabby, he was doing it because he was our older brother and he had to.

A lot of the teasing directed at me at school actually came from the adults. I think they found it funny there was such a tall kid in class and thought that meant they could make jokes about all of us kids. One teacher used to crack jokes about me all the time. I hated him. He had taught a number of my older siblings and, given we all admit to being bad students, he probably just hated anyone with Adams as their last name.

Not all the teachers were bad, though. I'll always remember Miss Walsh, who taught me in my early days at primary school and knew I had trouble learning at the same pace as everyone else. She was one of the only teachers who managed to be patient with me and actually give me a chance. I don't know if she was a good teacher for anyone else, but she showed me that it's okay to ask questions and to admit that you don't understand something. Even after she left the school she stayed in touch. She would email messages to the new teacher to pass on to me about how she saw my sister Valerie (Val) throwing the shot put on TV and asking if I had read any good books lately. I got embarrassed because other kids would mock me for getting emails from the teacher, so I acted too cool and didn't reply. But I always appreciated that she went out of her way to make me feel comfortable learning, as that was a big thing, especially at that time in my life.

It was about then that my parents split up. I must have been six or seven when Mum took me and Gabby to Tonga with her. I guess she wanted to have her kids with her, but Dad wouldn't let her take all of us so they split us up. I loved it there. It was hot all the time and I had a pet pig that I named Sitiveni, which is the Tongan version of my name. He wasn't a cute piglet like Babe, either. He was a fully grown pig that I used to ride on around the village. After maybe a couple of months, Gabby and I came back to New Zealand and moved in with Dad. We didn't see Mum for more than five years after that.

In Dad's house, his word was the law. And that law didn't just apply to his children, it applied to his wife too. No elbows on the table. No eating bread until you'd finished dinner. Always do your chores on time. Whatever Sid said went. As a father he was stern but fair. Everyone wanted to be on Dad's good side because he was the boss. At 6′11″ and with a barrel for a body, it was hard not to be intimidated by him, no matter who you were. By the time I was a teenager, his hair was white and he walked with a limp and a hunch. But that didn't make him any less imposing. He had a notorious work ethic among his co-workers and was always quick with a joke. But he would be the first one to admit that he wasn't a great husband. For Sid Adams, being a wife meant staying home, cooking and looking after the kids. He was always the boss in the relationship and he was possessive of his wife. He didn't like her going out socializing without him or someone else in his family to keep an eye on her. In his view it was the husband's job to earn money and put food on the table, which he did very well. And it was the wife's job to cook that food. These ideas sound pretty old-fashioned now, because they are. Remember, the dude was born in 1931.

Back at home with Dad, Gabby and I settled back into the routine. Because the house had only three bedrooms, the boys shared a room and the girls did too. Sid and I often turned our room into a wrestling ring by pushing our foam mattresses together and using the girls' mattresses to line the walls. We would use Gabby as our practice dummy for moves until she would get hurt and not want to play anymore. Sid was the best at it because he was the oldest, but he also seemed more naturally gifted than the rest of us. I was unco for my whole childhood. Being taller than other kids meant everyone assumed I was also going to be the toughest. That stopped the bullies from picking on me after a while, even though I wasn't any tougher, just longer.

The problem with being a head taller than everyone else is that people think you must be good at sports just because you're tall. I played a lot of sports as a kid, but I definitely wasn't good. My position in rugby was lock because that's where all the tall kids play, but the other teams soon found out that I couldn't catch the ball to save my life. I remember one game it felt like all the other team did was kick the ball to me, then I'd drop it and they'd score. We lost that game and I gave up hope of being an All Black.

I played basketball, of course, because you can't be a six-foot-tall 10-year-old and not play basketball. But I wasn't even in the top team at primary school. I was put in the B team with the other useless kids. My sister Gabby was the basketball player in the family. She got a scholarship to go and play basketball at a high school across town in Rotorua, which was rare in those days. I knew that three of my older brothers, Warren, Ralph, and Rob, had all been good basketball players, but I really only played because it was something to do after school. No one went to training or practiced—we just showed up at games in our muddy clothes and tried not to get hurt.

I never had a problem with my siblings, but they all seemed to have a problem with me. At least, that's what it felt like being the youngest and always getting picked on. I used to hear other kids at school talking about going to see their other friends after school and I'd wonder why they didn't just hang out with their brothers and sisters and their cousins. I thought everyone had a bunch of family members to play with every day, although I don't know if I'd describe what we did as "play." It always started out as playing, but because we're all so competitive it would quickly turn into a fight. When we played backyard cricket, someone would argue that they didn't get out when they were clearly out, or they wouldn't give the other person a turn for ages. One time, Sid got angry and broke the bat. Then we used an old metal pole until I threw it in the air and it hit Gabby in the forehead.

At some point Dad put up a basketball hoop and we started playing basketball. Two-on-two or one-on-one. Being the youngest and scrawniest, I lost every time, even against my sisters. *Especially* against my sisters. NBA fans like to say I'm tough, but none of my family would agree with them. In my family, I'm the weak youngest one who just happened to grow to be the tallest. Posting up against Lisa and Gabby when I was younger was way rougher than any player I mark in the NBA now. The only comeback I had against them was that if they ever got so pissed off that they wanted to smash me, I could usually run to Dad and then they couldn't do anything.

We all knew that Dad had a soft spot for me because I was the youngest, and I took full advantage of it. I could get away with things that no other Adams kid would dream of doing. The downside of that was that Sid, Lisa, and Gabby grew to be independent extremely young and went off to do their own things while I was still choosing to hang around with just Dad. It also meant that some of my much older brothers felt that since Dad wasn't being as tough on me as he was with them, it was their job to pick up the slack. If I answered back to my dad or didn't do as I was told, it wasn't him I had to look out for, it was my brothers.

Looking back, it's a small miracle we all ended up as sane, functioning members of society. Dad was over 65 when Mum left and suddenly he was a pensioner solo parent. The caring went both ways, though, because by that time he had a lot of health issues. While he looked after us and kept us out of trouble, we also cared for him. He was a heavy smoker for pretty much his whole life and only quit after I was born. As I grew taller, I noticed his age catching up with him and he started to hunch over when he walked. It almost seemed as if he was shrinking. Before any of us younger lot were born, Dad had been in a car crash with a drunk driver that mangled his lower legs. When I was growing up it was a normal part of the day for local nurses to stop by and change the bandages on his legs. He'd flirt with them because he was always a charmer, even as an old man. I wouldn't be surprised if a couple of them fell in love with him.

As each of us kids got old enough, we were taught how to change his dressings. Peeling off the bandages would reveal weeping flesh that looked like a shark or crocodile had attacked him. Then we'd have to use medical tissue to wipe away any pus that had oozed out before applying a fresh bandage. I can't say I enjoyed doing it, but it made me feel like I was being helpful and doing something for my dad that he couldn't do. We never found out what was actually wrong with his legs or why they never seemed to heal; it was just part of the routine.

As his legs got worse and his asthma flared up more frequently, Dad started spending more and more time inside. It was strange seeing him like that because he would usually have been outside knocking around in the garage or off in the van running errands. One of my most vivid memories of my dad is him sitting in our rust-bucket van with his massive arm out the window almost touching the ground. I swear he could have unscrewed the front wheel nuts from inside the car if he had wanted to.

The more Dad's health deteriorated, the more responsibilities we had to pick up. Sid learned how to drive when he was about 13, and even though he didn't have a license he'd drive us to basketball or to the supermarket. Lisa has always been the clever one, so she'd write up a shopping list and get the bank card off Dad and we'd all go to do the grocery shopping. It didn't feel like we were being forced to be adults. At least it didn't feel like that to me, but I usually just had to tag along and not get in the way. Even though we had access to Dad's money, we never took advantage of it by buying extra snacks or lollies. Instead we'd wait for Fridays, when we'd be given our allowance.

Dad would hand a crisp $10 note to Sid or Lisa and we'd all walk to a little block of shops on the corner of our road. Lisa would run into the liquor store, where the lady behind the counter knew all of us. She would split the note into coins and Lisa would give us each our share. It was like a mini hori business meeting. The next 30 minutes was when I would make the most important decisions of my childhood. Chocolates or gummies? Sour or not? Zombie Chews or seashells? We'd browse the pick 'n' mix counter at the local dairy for way too long before finally emerging holding a white paper bag stuffed with lollies.

One Friday I thought of a genius plan and waited until the others had walked back home. I bought a bunch of chocolate coins with my allowance and then walked to a different dairy to try to buy more lollies using the chocolate coins as currency. The dairy owner just laughed at me as I sulked off. That's when I wondered if maybe I wasn't as clever as I thought I was.

We certainly weren't left completely to our own devices. Viv and her kids lived fewer than 10 houses down from our house, and after Mum left, Viv took over a lot of the maternal duties. She had her own job and family to think about, but she always came down every few days to make sure everything was all right. Most of the time that meant just telling us off for not keeping the house tidy, but she usually brought food over or cooked us a feed. Every once in a while, she'd take all of us on a day out to the park or somewhere to give Dad some peace and quiet at home.

Even though most Adams kids were raised by a single parent, some by Dad, some by their mums, they saw me, Sid, Gabby, and Lisa as being different somehow because of how old and increasingly unwell Dad was. As we got older we started to see more and more of our older siblings, some of whom we didn't even know were related to us. Most of them stepped up to help in their own way and influenced me in ways I didn't even realize until recently. While Dad was our rock and our hero, some of the older siblings made sure we were behaving and going to school. It's a part of my story that the media overlooked when I first started getting their attention. Even though we lived a bit rugged, we were never alone. We always had people looking out for us. And one of those people was my brother Mohi.

Most of the Adams family met Mohi at my sister Gabby's seventh birthday party, which means I was six. We never had big birthday parties where we invited all our friends over; we just got the family together and had a feed. Mohi, who was 18 at the time, turned up and was casually introduced to us as our brother.

Dad was clearly in charge of all his relationships right from the beginning—you can tell just from the names of his children. Fourteen big, brown kids and we've all got the whitest names you've ever heard. Mohi's got a Māori name only because Dad didn't even know he was his kid until Mohi was older.

I think Viv had invited Mohi after finding out that he was one of Dad's kids but had been raised by his mum. Viv has always been the one responsible for wrangling all of the different Adams kids together. So there he was, another brother who I never knew existed but who was now part of the family. What my older siblings learned that day, and I found out later, was that Mohi was about 10 years old when he found out our dad was his dad. Dad used to visit his mum and would make sure his grades at school were good, but Mohi always thought he was just a friend. As it turns out, Dad and Mohi's mum were madly in love but were never able to get married. Mohi decided he'd like to meet some of his siblings so he got in touch with Viv and she invited him to our house for a birthday feed.

He's the only Adams son who didn't inherit the height genes from our dad. After Gabby's party I didn't see him around much. But what I did see about one morning a week was a bag full of Burger King on the kitchen table. I didn't even think to wonder how it got there, I just gladly ate the cheeseburgers and Whoppers. The Burger King deliveries continued for a couple of years and were then joined by bakery drop-offs and sometimes a random box of kiwifruit. Mohi worked at Burger King so after work he and his partner Matewai would drive by the house to drop off any leftover burgers. Mohi was still not sure about his relationship with Dad, let alone us, so he made the stops quick and late at night. I guess he saw my dad raising us alone and (correctly) assumed we could probably do with some more food.

Over the years, Mohi started making more appearances. Viv would invite him and Matewai to different family gatherings and they'd always show up, slowly integrating more into the family unit. It's tricky with a big family like ours, and one that has different "groups," because it's hard to tell how involved everyone wants to be with the other siblings outside their own group. I didn't really care either way.

That is, until I was about 10 and I found out that Mohi worked on a farm. There was something about farms that appealed to me even then. The thought of being out in the field putting in hard, physical work without having to write down any answers in a classroom sounded like a dream job. I was starting to really shoot up by then and I wanted to put my size to good use too, especially since I couldn't seem to play basketball as well as everyone had hoped.

The next time Mohi came by the house, I begged him to let me go to the farm with him. Dad just shrugged, so the next school holidays Matewai picked me up and I spent two of the best weeks of my life working on the farm with Mohi.

It was August and calving season. Our first proper outing on the farm didn't start well. We'd been out all day, with Mohi birthing the calves and his little kids and me wrangling them. The weather was terrible, and we were in a paddock near a dangerous cliff, but we were almost done for the day so were feeling good. The fence closest to the cliff had a gate, which was open, but because he was on the other side of the paddock and exhausted, Mohi told me to stand in the opening. "Just stay there and don't let the calf run by you," he instructed. I guess he figured since I was so big I could literally stand still and do the job. So along came the bull calf and the first thing it did was run straight at me. If you make a lot of noise and wave your arms, farm animals will almost always run away. But I didn't know that because I was a kid who'd never been to a farm before, so instead I did a little squeal and jumped out of the way. I still haven't lived it down.

Despite that crappy start to life on the farm, I fell in love with it over the next fortnight. Knowing that I was working and being useful made me want to get better and better at it. I think my dad had that same fight, and that's why he was such a force at the timber yard he worked in right up until he had to retire hurt.

I wasn't the only stray brother Mohi had picked up. He had three younger brothers on his mum's side, and since we were around the same age, Mohi figured we could hang out together and learn the meaning of putting in a hard day's work. The farm had a routine and I love routines. Every morning before sunrise Mohi would wake us and ask who wanted to work today. At the start it was compulsory, but after the first week we could just hang out at the house playing table tennis or go looking for swimming holes if we wanted to. I loved learning about the farm business, though, so I always said yes to the work.

Farming isn't easy but it's the most fulfilling work I've ever done. As well as helping with calving, we built fences, sorted the feed, and cleared land. I had assumed that farming was good for someone like me who didn't really like learning in a classroom but who had natural strength. I soon learned more about math and science then I ever had in school. When Mohi told me to calculate how much feed was needed for 450 cows, I had to make sure it was exactly right. Being 10 percent wrong either side meant wasting Mohi's money or underfeeding the cows.

When we were putting up fences and wiring them to be electrified, Mohi explained why each hole had to be dug a certain depth and why the wires had to be taut but not so tight that they would snap. We worked out the perfect angles so that the fence wouldn't collapse in a storm, and we learned how to wire the finished fences with electricity.

I soon found out that I learn best when concepts are explained to me using real-life applications. I would have been bored senseless learning about angles in class, but out in a paddock with Mohi explaining why a foundation post has to be at a 90-degree angle, it made sense pretty quick. I always had a lot of questions, which I'm sure got very annoying very fast. But I always like to know the reason behind doing something. That continues today and is why I ask coaches and trainers for the reason behind every play, drill, or workout.

Perhaps the best part about working on the farm with Mohi was that at the end of the day we could look out and see everything we'd accomplished. It's rare to spend a day working on a farm and not have any visible progress to show for your efforts.

One of the best things was that every night Matewai would put on a mean feed. We always had enough food at home with Dad, but dinner tastes a little sweeter when you've been out in the cold working hard all day. What I realized only recently, after doing my own food shopping, was that having four boys staying for two weeks must have at least tripled their food bill. We had free milk and free meat from the farm, but Matewai has since told me they would spend an extra $1,000 on food for those two weeks that we stayed. That in itself should've been enough reason to never let us stay again, but it didn't put them off. After that first holiday, I couldn't wait to go back. For the next three years, every school holiday and most long weekends I'd get picked up by Matewai and spend time on the farm.

In those three years I kept growing at a fairly rapid pace. By the time I was 12, I was well over 6 feet tall and I had size 16 feet. Do you know how hard it is to find size 16 gumboots? It's damn near impossible. So in the summer, when it wasn't icy, I'd farm barefoot. I must have looked ridiculous. This lanky kid walking through mud and cow shit all day in his bare feet. Matewai would be constantly growling at me for bringing shit into the house either on my feet or clothes. I would just walk in and flop myself down on the couch until Matewai would come charging over and shoo me towards the shower. That time spent out with Mohi and Matewai did me a lot of good. I'd be exhausted at the end of every day, which, for a kid who was usually bouncing off the walls, was a rare feat.

I'm still not entirely sure why Mohi and Matewai took it upon themselves to take me in for those few years. I don't think Dad asked them to, but he definitely appreciated it. When I was 10 years old, Dad was 70. He'd taught Sid a lot of things that dads teach their sons. How to fix things and use power tools and look after his younger siblings. But by the time I was old enough to learn, Dad was tired. He couldn't come outside and play with me or teach me how to use a chainsaw or anything like that. So that's where Mohi stepped in.

He was certainly strict, and there was no swearing or slacking off. I did more dishes for Mohi and Matewai than I ever did at home. It took a little while to get used to it, but once I knew what the boundaries were, I stayed within them.

Whether he realized it or not, Mohi was like my second dad. He was only 24 the first time he let me stay, younger than I am now. I was his helper around the farm and soaked up everything he said. He taught me how to ride a farm bike and then banned me from ever riding one after I bent the handlebars. And he made me want to do a good job for him so much that I ended up hurting myself because of it.

We were putting up a fence on one of my later visits and Mohi had me hold up a wooden board that he needed to nail in. We'd done it a dozen times before and I knew the most important thing was to hold it perfectly still, which meant pushing it hard against the post. I grabbed the board and pressed my knee against it for extra stability as he started hammering. I could feel the impact shock going through my leg every time he made contact with the nail.

What I wasn't expecting was for the shock to get worse. It actually started properly hurting. "Hey Mohi," I said between hits. "It's starting to hurt." He just shook his head and kept hammering. The pain only got worse with each hit. "Mohi, it really hurts."

"Shut up, I'm almost done," he growled, and gave the nail one last hammer before he stood up. I pulled my leg away from the board and we both saw that Mohi had hammered the nail straight through the post and into my thigh. Mohi tried to act like it was some sort of rite of passage, but I didn't buy it. Luckily, I hadn't started crying. Rightly or wrongly, being able to take a punch was regarded highly in my family. It's a skill that's harder to master when you're the youngest, but I think it's fair to say that it has served me well since.

I might have been only 12 years old at that point, but I was planning out my whole life. I'd get a paid job on a farm as soon as I could, then save up to buy my own land. Mohi worked as a manager on someone else's farm, so we would always talk about what I had to do in order to run my own farm and not have to work for someone else. By starting work young, I could help my dad out with some of the bills and pay him back for all he'd done. Maybe I'd go on a business course to polish up on that side of things before getting my farm set up. I knew exactly what I was going to do with the rest of my life.

And then Dad got sick.

2.

DAD GETS SICK

No one knows for sure how many kids my dad had. If you ask anyone in the media they'll say he had 18, or maybe even 20, but they won't know where that number came from. If you ask my sister Viv, she'll say it's 16. I always thought there were 14 of us. Whatever the number, there will only ever be one Sid Adams.

Dad joined the merchant navy straight out of school in Bristol, England, and a few years later, when the boat he was working on docked in the Bay of Plenty, he jumped ship. He ended up in Rotorua and never left. Almost as soon as he arrived in New Zealand he shacked up with a local woman and had two daughters. The relationship clearly wasn't a great one because those two daughters chose to have nothing to do with him for the rest of his life. Unfazed, he hung around, driving logging trucks for a forestry company and apparently meeting plenty of women.

In 2005, when I was 12 years old, Viv and Valerie organized an Adams family reunion. It was going to be the first complete Adams reunion ever. It would also be the last. Maybe they waited until they were sure Dad wasn't going to have any more kids before trying to round us all up. Or maybe they wanted to make sure none of us were accidentally dating our cousin, seeing as quite a few of us kids hadn't properly met. The reunion was held at our house and almost everyone showed up: 13 kids, with some getting to know each other properly for the first time.

Even though some of the brothers, like Mohi and Rob, only found out they were Dad's kids later on in life, as soon as they were introduced to us it was like they'd been there the whole time. Looking around, it wasn't hard to tell we all came from the same guy. You couldn't turn anywhere without bumping into a giant Adams forehead. I think Mohi might be the only one who escaped the famous Adams brow.

It was cool seeing Val again. She'd been competing all around the world in shot put and had just come third at the world champs. She was definitely the star of the family, but because she had grown up and lived in Auckland, I didn't feel that connected to her. She was more of a distant sister who we sometimes would see on TV. Yet Val's upbringing wasn't all that different from ours and it seemed like the two of us actually had a lot in common. She's the tallest girl of the family at 6'4", and although at that age I didn't look tall standing next to her, I was on my way to becoming the tallest boy. At that reunion, though, Ralph and Warren, both nearly 7 feet tall, were the big brothers in every way.

I looked at Val and all she was achieving on her own and couldn't help but be impressed. Even though at that point I wasn't taking anything seriously, and definitely not basketball, she showed me that the Adams family definitely had the talent and the genes; we just had to put in a bit of hard work and we'd go far. Ralph and Warren also had the genes and talent. Quite a few people over the years have said they could have been in the NBA if that had been an option for New Zealanders in the 1980s.

Viv has always been the photographer of the family and even now her house is packed with photo albums and framed photos of us all. She went around that day and got all of Dad's "lots" in photos with him. First it was the older lot with Viv. Then Rob on his own and Mohi on his own, followed by Val's team. Then finally Sid, Lisa, Gabby, and me. The photos aren't fancy at all, just taken on Viv's cheap digital camera, but they're the only proper family photos we have with Dad. Then it was decided we had to all appear in a photo together.

Having 14 people in a photo is a bit of a mission if they're a normal size. But Adams kids aren't a normal size. Viv thought it would be cool to have us all in height order so we all argued for a bit over who was shorter than who, then formed a line. Dad was right in the middle. He would've been closer to the tall end if he could still stand up straight, but it worked out perfectly for the photo. Because I was only 12, I was still the shortest, or at least pretty close to the shortest next to Viv, so I was right down at one end. We got one of the partners to take the photo and we should have known then it was a mistake, because she was a foot shorter than most of us, so the angles were all wrong from the beginning. After a lot of pushing and shoving we all stood still for the one second it took to take a single photo and that was it. No one bothered to check if the photo was all right; we just wanted to stop having to pose like idiots.

When the photo was processed, we all saw that I'd been cut

off along with our sister Marg. Not even a little bit cut off or half cut off, just completely removed. We still laugh about it when we get together, but it kinda sucks that it is the only photo that exists of all of us with Dad. And I'm not even in it.

Not long after that reunion, Dad found out he was dying. Of course, he didn't tell me at first.

I knew Dad was going to the doctor because he had fairly regular checkups for his legs and his asthma. When he got home I asked if there was anything wrong. He told me the doctor had found "some white stuff in my stomach." I thought they must have just seen the ice cream we'd eaten earlier swirling around in his tummy. I told him that and he nodded, which to me meant he was fine.

That night, Viv came by the house as she always did, and she and Dad sat in the lounge talking. When Dad had gone to bed, Viv called me, Sid, Gabby, and Lisa out to the living room. "Dad's sick," she said. "He's really sick. He's got cancer." I knew what cancer was and I knew it wasn't just ice cream swirling around in his tummy. Viv explained how the doctors didn't think there was much they could do and Dad, being Dad, didn't want to go through all the chemotherapy and radiation, so he was just going to wait it out.

I started to think of it as just another health problem that Dad would have to live with. He'd had asthma and his gammy legs for as long as I could remember, and now he'd have cancer. It would just be another part of the daily routine. But when I saw how upset Lisa and Gabby were, I started to realize that it was serious. Viv didn't know how long he had left, but we all thought it would be, at worst, just a few years.

After our little meeting we ran to Dad and hugged him. By that point we were all crying, which he didn't like. "Stop the bloody crying," he said, the first of many times he would say that. "I'm the one who should be crying, not you guys." It was typical Dad, telling his kids off for crying over something even if it was the news that he was dying. Viv told us later that when he told her he was sick he laughed as if it was the world's funniest joke. That was just Dad; he always had a bit of a dark sense of humor.

Everything moved so quickly after that and no one, even now, can remember exactly how long he was sick. At one point, Viv took him to the hospital for a procedure which they stuffed up. I guess it was a colonoscopy because they burst something up there. They sent him home anyway because he didn't complain about the pain.

But a few days later he was in agony, so he called Viv and asked her to leave work to drive him to the hospital. When she asked him why he didn't just call the ambulance, he said he didn't want to pay the fee for getting an ambulance pickup. If you ever hear me being a tight arse and complaining about paying for parking, that's where I get it from.

Once Dad was back in hospital, he stayed there. Viv came by every morning and night to make sure we were going to school and had something to eat for dinner. She also called Mum in Tonga and told her to come back because Dad was sick. She did come back, but it didn't feel right. She got a job working at night and we barely saw her, which suited us kids just fine since that's what we were used to. It felt weird to have my own mum living in the same house as me and feeling like a stranger. During that time, Viv felt like more of a mother simply because she'd been helping out for so long and wasn't about to stop just because Mum was back on the scene.

Life continued on as normal, or as normal as it could be. Sid was 17 by then, working and doing his own thing. He became the full-time driver and also a fill-in dad for us while Dad was in hospital. He'd drive us all to basketball trainings and to school if it was raining, then help get dinner sorted when he got home from work. It all seemed natural and normal at the time, but Sid had to grow up real fast once Dad got sick.

All the siblings from around the country came to visit Dad while he was sick. Val came down from Auckland every week-end that she could, and Warren and Ralph flew in to see Dad, but then had to go back to work.

Eventually, we got word from the nurses at the hospital that Dad could come home. He couldn't even walk at that point and he had lost a lot of weight, but they thought he would be more comfortable at home. We all agreed, and it was arranged for a hospital bed to be delivered so we could set it up in the lounge for him. We all knew it would be his final move, but we were so happy at the thought of him being back in the lounge where we had been used to seeing him our whole lives. If you're from a big family, or an island family (usually those two go together), you'll know what it's like to "visit" a sick relative in the hospital. It's not really about sitting down and talking to them, most of the time you're just hanging out with your cousins and mucking around *near* the sick person. That's exactly what we were doing when Dad got worse.

I still don't know what exactly happened, but suddenly he wasn't allowed to come home. Viv sent one of her daughters to go get Gabby from basketball practice and then called Ralph and Warren, who had both just flown home, and told them to hurry back because Dad was on his way out. It was a Monday.

By Tuesday everyone except Val was back in Rotorua. She had been at an athletics meet and was in Sydney on her way home when Viv told her the news. Everyone was freaking out and wondering what had gone wrong with Dad. One minute he was supposed to be going home with us and the next he was barely able to talk or move. As kids we thought the nurses or doctors must have done something wrong for him to get worse. It took a few hours before we stopped blaming the hospital staff and started thinking maybe Dad had just had enough. Perhaps he had given up or just decided it was his time to go.

Within 24 hours every one of the Adams kids was back except Val, but Dad was deteriorating quickly. He couldn't move or talk or even make noises. His hands, those enormous hands, lay motionless at his sides. When I put my hand in his and squeezed, he didn't squeeze back. There was a rumor around town that Dad had once broken a guy's hand by squeezing it too hard in a handshake. I started wishing he would break my hand in his grip because at least that meant he could still move. But instead his hands just lay there, huge and calloused from a long life of labor.

By the next morning, the older siblings were starting to worry that Val wouldn't make it back in time. Dad had gotten worse, to the point where we had to keep sponging his mouth because he couldn't swallow. Every kid thinks their parents are invincible, especially their dad. We were the same, except our dad was 6'11", huge and strong, so we had even more reason to believe that he couldn't die. Seeing him so helpless and unable to fight off whatever was killing him was almost too much for me. I couldn't even comprehend that my big, strong, grumpy dad was lying helpless in a bed. It didn't make any sense. He could do anything—and now he couldn't even breathe on his own.

Having all of our older siblings there was a good distraction. People were coming in and out of the hospital room all day. Someone would go on a food run and I'd tag along. Or we'd go outside with the cousins and run around for a bit. But any time one of us went back into the room and saw Dad, it hit us again. We'd have a cry together and then someone would crack a joke and we'd be laughing but still kind of crying. I started spending more and more time out in the waiting area just to avoid seeing Dad so frail. Back in the room we would over-analyze every little noise or twitch he made. Was he trying to smile? Was he trying to tell us something?

Val was due to arrive in Auckland that afternoon and was going to race down to Rotorua, a three-hour drive away. We all kept telling Dad to hold on just a little longer because Val was the last one to come. If he could just hold on, he could go surrounded by all his kids.

Val arrived at 8 p.m. We let her have some time alone with Dad before all 14 of us joined her around his bed. The doctors had already told us that he would go that night, so even though he was in intensive care, where there are strict visiting hours, we were allowed to be there all day and into the night. Hospital rooms are tiny, so having all 14 of us in there, plus my siblings' kids, meant we were all squashed up. Then we waited.

Every few moments someone would tell a story about Dad or crack a joke that would have us all giggling, but mostly we just watched and waited. I never thought I'd ever want my dad to die, but after seeing him struggling so much those last few days, I just wanted him to be at peace. It's weird to stand there and wait for heartbreak. I'd never taken a second in my life to consider what I would do if Dad died and suddenly there I was, waiting for Dad to die. And, of course, being Dad, he had to make it dramatic.

All of us had our eyes glued to his massive chest as it would slowly rise and fall with each breath. After about an hour, he took a really long breath and his chest puffed out real big, and then it stopped. I heard someone sob and I thought that was it, he was gone. But then a second later he breathed out and his chest deflated. We were all coming back from that moment when we noticed his chest hadn't risen again, and the emotions came out again. And then he breathed again! Honestly, it was like he was playing one last game with us.

He did that a few more times before some of the older brothers grumbled that he was just pissing around now, which made us all laugh. They had a point. Here we were trying to prepare for the worst moment of our lives and it was like Dad couldn't make up his mind whether to stay or go. Then it messed with us because we started to think that maybe those long breaths meant he was fighting through it. Maybe he was the one in a million who beats the odds.

It must've sounded ridiculous to all the nurses and anyone else in the ward. It was ten o'clock at night and this massive family was crying and then laughing and then crying and laughing again. I don't know if it's a brown thing, but if you're not laughing at the hospital, no matter what the situation, you're doing it wrong.

When it finally happened, it was somehow a surprise and a relief at the same time. We all broke down. Someone, or maybe more than one person, started screaming. The nurses came by with tissues and words of comfort. When someone came in to check he had really passed, everyone except for Viv had to leave the room. That's when we knew he was really gone.

We'd been crying for weeks but Dad had always been sick, so it was easy to believe that the sickness would never beat him. We thought that we'd grow up and have to look after him, like we were supposed to. When I think back now, it's amazing he lived so long with all the health issues he had. I like to think he fought until his youngest kids were all in their teens and could maybe look out for themselves.

He pushed us out as far as he could before resting, and I'll always be thankful for that.

Dad took his final breath at 10:56 p.m. on 2 May 2007. It was a Wednesday.

3.

THE FUNERAL

Every culture does funerals differently. Some are pretty boring if I'm honest, and usually start and finish on the day of the service. Dad was white, but none of his kids were. So instead of trying to decide between a Tongan, Māori, or Tokelauan funeral, we just made up our own version.

When we walked back into the house after leaving the hospital there was still a space cleared in the lounge for Dad's hospital bed. We designated that spot to be where he would rest until the burial. I guess he was still coming home that week after all, just not how we thought.

Things got hectic trying to prepare the house for the service. I don't know who made the decision to hold the funeral in our lounge, but it made sense. Dad was never religious and would have hated a church service. The lounge was his church.

Sid, Gabby, Lisa, and I just did what we were told—cleaning our rooms or going with someone older to pick up mattresses for everyone to sleep on. The boys' room and girls' room suddenly had to accommodate a lot more boys and girls. I don't think anyone slept in Dad's room, that would have been too weird.

When Dad came home early the next morning, none of us had slept. I'd never stayed awake that long in my life, but I didn't want to sleep in case I missed something. I didn't want to waste any of the last moments I'd have with Dad. In Tongan, Māori, and most Pacific cultures, the custom is to have your loved one rest at home before the burial. Each culture does it slightly differently, but the one thing they all have in common is the belief that the loved one should never be alone. None of us were ready to leave Dad's side anyway, so we covered the floor of the lounge with mattresses and people could get some sleep while they were with him. He was home and in his favorite spot surrounded by his kids.

As word got out that Sid Adams had passed away, people started dropping in to pay their respects. I had always known Dad to be quite standoffish with anyone who wasn't family, so I didn't think he had many friends. But he obviously had made an impression on everyone he met because it seemed like the whole town passed through our house to say goodbye. Extended family, school groups, workers at the timber yard, basketball people, even those who owned the dairy and the liquor store down the road came through.

It was almost exciting to see all these people who knew Dad and had stories about him from before we were born. Everyone knew our house was Sid Adams's house, so even if you were just driving past you probably could figure out what had happened. So many people passed through that we were all too busy making sure everyone was welcomed and fed to process our own loss just yet. But whenever there was a quiet moment without visitors, when it was just us and Dad, that's when it would start to sink in.

We sat on those mattresses next to Dad and talked for hours, sharing stories about him and how different he was for each of us. My oldest brothers talked about how he was so much tougher on them when they were young. Dad was too old to be handing out any hidings by the time I came along, but I would have preferred a couple of smacks over what I got instead, which was the disappointed voice. That would knock me out for days. I can handle the physical stuff, no sweat. It's the thought of letting people down that gets me stressed out.

It's a shame that it took Dad's death to bring all of us together again, because having everyone there supporting each other made all the difference. I didn't do much in the days after Dad died—just hung around the house watching all these people I didn't know come to say hello and goodbye to the old man.

On the day of the funeral we dressed up flash and cleaned up the lounge for the service. We mostly held it so that we could say our own goodbyes, forgetting how popular Dad was. People kept showing up until the lounge was packed, so we opened the doors out to the front yard. Then that filled up and people ended up down the driveway and having to stand on the footpath outside our gate. No one outside of the lounge would have been able to hear anything, but they didn't seem to mind. All that mattered was that they were there. We could hardly believe it.

The service was short, which was good since Dad looked a little bit cramped in his coffin. He might have lost a lot of weight before he died, but he was still a massive guy. An extra-long coffin had to be custom-made for him, but it was a tiny bit narrow so he looked like he was hunched into it. A snug coffin seemed strangely fitting for a guy who had always been larger than life.

When it was time to put the lid on the coffin, it really hit Val hard. None of us were ready to see Dad for the last time, but Val jumped forward and put her arm across him, stopping whoever was about to close the coffin. Ralph, Warren, and Rob (who are all over 6'9") rushed to comfort her but ended up fighting to restrain her. Gabby and I were watching, wondering why Val hated the coffin lid guy so much, and why she suddenly decided to fight three brothers at once. I wasn't old enough to see it for the show of grief that it was.

No one else dared get involved. If any of us had accidentally walked into one of Val's swinging arms, we would've been out for the count, no doubt about it. In fact, if it weren't for my three older brothers, I reckon Val could've taken on all of us that day, *Royal Rumble* style. Instead, Ralph, Warren, and Rob managed to subdue her, the lid was placed over the coffin, and I saw my dad and best friend for the last time.

At the burial we formed a circle around Dad's grave as he was being lowered into the ground. Next to the grave was a pile of flowers and wreaths that had been left by mourners at the service. We all grabbed some flowers and said our goodbyes as we threw them onto the lowered coffin. It was silent and emotional, and everyone was crying until we heard a loud thud that sounded as though Dad was knocking from inside the coffin. We all jumped, only to see that Sid had thrown in an entire pot plant. It was so random and dumb that we all cracked up. To anyone standing further away, it probably looked like we were huddled together sobbing, but really we were all laughing at Sid. Those random moments didn't seem like much at the time, but I now see they kept me going on the worst day of my life.

Afterwards, the house suddenly felt too big. The lounge had way too much space in it and, even though it was still full of mattresses and people, it felt weirdly quiet. In the years to come I slowly came to understand that the emptiness I felt was grief and the loneliness of living without Dad.

Things had moved fast when Dad got sick, but everything suddenly slowed down after his burial. The older siblings had to get back to their jobs and families, so the fantastic four were back to being the only ones at home. I didn't think all my siblings would be sticking around, and they had only been at the house for a few days, but I'd already gotten used to having a crowded house. Suddenly, the four of us in a three-bedroom home seemed like not nearly enough people.

Mum was still around, and I recall her being at the funeral, but for some reason when I remember that time, she's not really in the picture. I imagine it must have been hard for her to come back and immediately be the sole parent of four kids she hadn't seen in half a decade, but she got no sympathy from us. As far as we were concerned, she'd only come back to her kids because she had to, and she was only sticking around out of obligation. Instead of being the parent we had in Dad, she felt more like a flatmate who we barely saw.

Everyone was telling me to go back to school, but to me school seemed pointless. The only reason I went to school before was because Dad would have told me off if I didn't. Now that Dad was gone, there was nothing stopping me from just staying home. I don't think I'm unique. Most 13-year-olds, even the ones who are good at school, wouldn't necessarily go if there was no one forcing them to.

So instead I stayed home and played video games. And, without meaning to brag, I got pretty good. If it's true that it takes 10,000 hours of practice to be an expert at something, I was definitely on my way to becoming an expert gamer. Some kids who lose a parent might get sent to grief counseling. I just played video games. I don't know if it actually worked, but it did stop me from thinking about Dad every second of every day. Sometimes Viv would stop by the house and see me there during the day. She'd tell me off and send me on my way, but then she'd have to go to work and I would just walk back home.

I didn't go back to stay with Mohi and Matewai on the farm after the funeral. Instead, my eldest brother, Barry, started coming by the house and keeping an eye on me. Barry worked as a truck driver and would take me on a few jobs with him in his truck. It was good to get out of the house for a while, but I didn't enjoy it as much as I did farming.

What I didn't know at the time is that Mohi and Matewai were looking into legally adopting me and having me live with them on the farm. I think if they'd given me that option, I would have jumped at it because home wasn't what it used to be.

Sid was 18 and off working full-time trying to pay the bills, Lisa had a boyfriend so was always busy, and Gabby was clashing a lot with Mum so had gone to stay with Viv. I wasn't old enough to be completely independent but still old enough that people didn't feel they had to babysit me. So I just existed in the house by myself.

When I think back I realize that I was actually very lonely and, if I'm honest, probably a little depressed. No one had told us how to cope with grief. We didn't see a counselor or go to any therapy sessions. After a while, Gabby, Lisa, and I would sometimes talk about Dad and tell stories about him or say how much we missed him. But Sid was tough; you couldn't talk about your feelings with him because he had other worries, like bringing in money to feed everyone.

In the summer after Dad died, Mum got me a job at a kiwifruit packing company. They weren't supposed to hire anyone under the age of 16, but because I was so tall I guess no questions were asked. It was only a weekend job, but it was my first ever paid work and I took it seriously.

Mum and I would drive there before sunrise and I'd spend 12 hours packing kiwifruit into boxes. It was super boring, but it was a job and I liked to do it well. At the end of the weekend $213 would be transferred into my bank account, a small fortune for a 13-year-old who never got more than a $2.50 allowance.

As soon as I got paid I'd rush to the ATM and take out $20 and spend it all on fish and chips. In Rotorua in 2007 you could get a lot of fish and chips for 20 bucks. I'd grab a couple of the neighborhood boys who I would sometimes run around with and we'd eat the feast together. It was the first time in my life I was able to provide food for myself and for someone else, and I loved how it felt.

I decided then that I'd make sure I could take care of myself as soon as possible.

4.

A SECOND CHANCE

You could say my NBA career plan started at a Christmas family barbecue in Rotorua when I was 13 years old. We had gone to Viv's place for a feed and Warren was up from Wellington. He asked how everyone was doing and we all mumbled that we were doing fine. He asked if I was still playing basketball and I said, "Yeah, kinda." He was looking me up and down, noticing for the first time how tall I'd grown.

"You want to play basketball seriously?" he asked. I had never even thought about it. My plan was still to become a farmer. But even though I didn't pay any attention to the NBA, or even local basketball, I knew that professional basketball players got paid a lot of money. And if there was one thing that was going to motivate me to pursue a career in something it would be the money, because not having enough was the cause of all the arguments I'd heard between my dad and siblings. I nodded to Warren, deciding on the spot that since I wasn't doing much else, I could probably handle going to basketball practice a bit more. He just nodded back and carried on eating. It wasn't a big revelation or discussion, nothing ever is in our family, but it set the wheels in motion.

I started going to basketball practice even though I still wasn't going to school. Doug Courtney, the Rotorua rep team coach, found some adidas shoes at a flea market that were size 16 and gave them to me. They were pretty much my only pair of shoes so I wore them everywhere—to trainings, school if I decided to go a couple of days, even on the farm.

Doug told me that I should go down to Wellington for a basketball trial. It was for some rep team that he was coaching, but once again I didn't really pay much attention beyond the fact that I was going to Wellington, a place I'd never been before.

When you're a kid you're supposed to do whatever adults tell you to do. The adult in my life was my dad, and once he was gone I wasn't sure if that meant I should be making my own decisions now. I decided that for the time being I'd listen to the adults around me, so when Doug Courtney said there was a basketball camp in Wellington and he'd take me, the only option was to say yes.

Well, the camp sucked. Actually, no, the camp didn't suck. Everyone there, from the coaches to the players to the management, was really good. I was the only one who sucked. I might have been tall, but that was about it. For the first time I had to train with other guys who were nearly the same height as me, but they had been training regularly for years. That weekend I got yelled at more than I'd been yelled at my entire life. Coaches were shouting out drills, which somehow everyone knew how to do except me. The other players were yelling at me, trying to tell me where to stand for every play.

Although I was the tallest on the court, I did shoot some three-pointers, which I'm sure everyone hated.

I didn't enjoy that camp. It wasn't that I didn't like playing basketball, I was just so far behind on basketball knowledge and that was the first time it became obvious. My drill partner for most of the trainings was a tall guy named Chris McIntyre, who was mean to me the whole weekend. We were complete opposites in every way. He was smart and did everything exactly how it was supposed to be done. I was grubby and had long hair that didn't look anywhere near as good as my long hair looks now.

I spent most of the camp just trying to swat every single shot. I didn't know what was happening on offense so instead I made it my mission to not let anyone score against me. I hung around the bottom of the key (the free-throw lane beneath the basket) and goal tended. It worked out well enough because I made sure every block was exaggerated. At one point, a power forward named Victor must have thought my useless offense meant I didn't know how to use my height, because he tried to drive around me. The ball ended up at the far end of the court next to us and he didn't try it again.

That's how basketball is when you're a kid. Being tall means you only have to be half as good to get by. But after getting bumped around by Gabby, Lisa, and Sid on our driveway basketball court for years, I knew that pretty soon just being tall wouldn't be enough.

As we drove back to Rotorua and to my regular life of video games and not much else, I thought about how hard the camp had been. I wasn't invited there because they expected me to be the best, and yet it pissed me off that I was maybe the worst.

My natural competitiveness started firing up and I was suddenly determined to not be so out of my depth if I was ever asked back to another trial. I knew there was no way I'd make the team, whatever team that was, and felt a little embarrassed about it.

I didn't find out until much later that the camp wasn't actually a trial. It was the New Zealand under 17 team having their training camp before they went to the Australian state champs. There wasn't even a chance that I could have made the team because it had been selected months earlier, which just goes to show how much I was paying attention to what was happening around me in those days.

But while I was settling back into my life of relaxing and eating, the people around me were sorting out my future.

Warren called Viv around March 2008 to follow up on his question about my basketball future. Was I really interested in pursuing it? Viv honestly didn't know, but in her mind me playing basketball was still better than me playing Xbox. She told Warren if he was willing to look after me in Wellington and get me into basketball, he should come and fetch me. I don't even remember being asked if I wanted to move to Wellington, so maybe I didn't have a choice in the matter. But I think if they had asked me, I would have said yes because I was starting to get bored at home.

Being bored for a day when you're 14 is fine. But being bored with life, like I was at 14, sucks. Sitting at home by myself all day made it easy for bad thoughts to seep in, and I'd find myself thinking about Dad constantly and how I was all alone now.

All I remember is being told that Warren was coming to pick

me up to take me to Wellington and then two days later he was there. That's how things worked in my family. There were never big meetings where we all discussed the options and decided together. Things just happened, and usually quickly. I wouldn't be where I am today if two of my siblings hadn't decided over one phone call that I should move to a different city, away from most of my family, and start a new life there.

When it came time to pack my bags I realized that I didn't own anything. I had one pair of basketball shoes, two pairs of shorts, a handful of T-shirts, and a few pairs of underwear. I didn't like reading so I had no books. We couldn't afford the gadgets or toys other kids had so I didn't have to pack any of that stuff. And while I loved gaming, the Xbox belonged to everyone so I wasn't about to try walking off with it. Warren had told me to pack up my life and it turned out my life could fit inside a sports bag.

Sid ended up coming with us on the trip to Wellington. At the time I thought he was just bored and wanted a change of scenery, but I've since learned that he came because he knew I'd need a familiar face in Wellington. Sid might have been rough with me as a kid and wasn't the best at expressing his love, but dropping everything to move cities to make sure I wasn't messed with? That's a real brother right there.

When we arrived, Warren took me straight to the Winter Show Buildings in Newtown to meet someone. I recognized the place from the training camp a few months earlier, which was reassuring. From the outside it looked like a giant garden shed, and inside it wasn't much better. There were two full-sized basketball courts with a few small bleachers along the baseline of each one, but mostly it looked like two training courts and

nothing more. Since then there have been some really good basketball arenas built around Wellington, but at that time a lot of
regional tournaments were held at the Show Buildings, even
though one of the hoops was clearly lower than the others.

As we walked across the courts with their random dead spots
and cracks, it felt unfamiliar. To me, it was just another gym with
just another group of kids training and just another coach yelling
out drills. That coach was an African American guy with a thick
accent who wore a hoodie, with the hood up, and sweatpants. He
was sitting on one of the player benches and occasionally yelling
out shooting drills to the kids who were training. He was yelling
loudly so everyone could hear him, but he wasn't mad or stressed.
And he didn't stand up unless he had to show someone a particular
move. Even before I properly met him, I knew this guy had swag.

Warren walked me over and the coach looked me up and
down. I could tell he was trying to figure out at first glance if
I was worth coaching. "Kenny, this is my brother Steven," said
Warren. "Steven, this is Kenny McFadden." I didn't say anything,
but then I didn't say much at all in those days. Kenny looked at
me and put up his hand for a high-five. I hesitated for a second
while I gawked at his raised hand. The ring finger was crooked.
And not just a little bit crooked but completely bent sideways at
the second knuckle. After a second, I slapped his hand and our
introduction was complete.

Warren and Kenny continued to chat while I zoned out and
watched the older guys work through their shooting drills. I
snapped back into the conversation when Kenny started talking
about training. He sounded like he was keen to train me, but only
if I was willing to put in as much work as he was. I'd never said

no to someone with a plan before and I wasn't about to start, so I said yes. If he was going to help me I was going to work hard and do whatever was needed. Kenny looked at me, nodded, and said, "That's good."

I went back to watching better players than me work on their skills. I watched them and couldn't wait to be as good as them, while next to me my brother and new coach planned out my new life.

The problem with doing whatever anyone tells you to do is that once people stop telling you to do things, you do nothing. When we got to Warren's place in Wainuiomata, on the outskirts of Wellington, my bed was the couch. I didn't mind, though, because I could, and still can, sleep anywhere.

Warren had planned for me to enroll at Wainuiomata High School because it was near his house and I could walk there on my own. But because I had barely been to school in two years, I didn't have any academic record so I couldn't be enrolled. While Warren was trying to sort out how and where I could go to school, I lapsed back into doing nothing. I just stayed home and watched TV—exactly what I was doing in Rotorua, except now I didn't have anyone to hang out with. The excitement I felt about moving cities and starting something new ended pretty quickly when I found myself going through the same routines I'd had back home. I thought maybe that's just what my life would be: do nothing, move to another place, do nothing there, move to another place, and on until I died. Even as a 14-year-old I didn't like the thought of just "hanging out" until I died.

While Warren had agreed that I would train with Kenny,

I wasn't. Not because I didn't want to, but because I couldn't. It would take 40 minutes to drive from Warren's house to the courts for the 6:30 a.m. training every morning. Even if Warren could make that drive before going to work, I had no way of getting home at 8 a.m. when training finished. Kenny lived on the other side of town so him coming to collect me wasn't an option either. My new life and career plan was put on hold while Warren and Kenny tried to figure out a solution. I'd traveled hundreds of kilometers to get into basketball, but it was the last 30 kilometers that were the real problem.

While I was waiting for things to happen, and starting to wonder if they ever would, an old friend of Warren's named Blossom told him I could train with her school team if I had nothing better to do. The team trained in the morning too, but she said she could drive me there and take me home afterwards. I assumed that meant she lived in Wainuiomata so I agreed to go along and train with her Scots College team until my situation with Kenny was sorted out.

At the first training, I learned quickly that the Scots College players weren't nearly as good as the ones I'd seen training with Kenny. But even though they weren't that great, they were all there at 6:30 a.m. working their arses off and trying to improve. I knew that these guys were like me, on the basketball court at least. I'd soon learn that their lives as private school students were about as far from mine as humanly possible, but on that basketball court we were all the same.

The boys respected Blossom. It's hard not to respect a ripped former bodybuilder with dreads and a half-shaved head, even if she is only 5 feet tall.

During that first training I was paired up with a guy called Pat. He was their big man, only he wasn't that big. He was stocky, though, and could throw his weight around. With my height advantage and his strength advantage we were a pretty good match-up.

After the training, Blossom dropped me home. It wasn't until the next week that I learned she didn't live in Wainuiomata at all. Once she had dropped me off, she drove the full 40 minutes back to Scots College, where she lived just a few minutes away.

She was about to become a crucial person in helping me to go from a boy who was happy wasting his days in front of an Xbox to a professional sportsman.

5.
NEW KID IN TOWN

People often don't believe that I started playing basketball properly as a teenager. Sports writers and experts always go on about how you can tell if a kid will become a professional athlete by the time they're nine, or something crazy like that. By the time you get to be 14, the kids who are really good are easy to spot and those who aren't start dropping off. I didn't know any of this back then because I never read any books about sport (or any books full stop), so I went in thinking it was completely normal for me to start my basketball career at 14 years of age.

Life in Wellington quickly turned into life with Blossom. There wasn't a big move, like my move to Wellington. She simply offered to put me up the night before morning training and drop me home the next night. This happened a few times and seemed to work, so then I stayed a few nights a week and started training with Kenny when there were no Scots College trainings. I still wasn't going to school, but I was getting up early and working out, so I felt I was at least making progress in one area of my life. Pretty soon I was staying almost every night with Blossom and within a month I was living at her place full-time. After spending my whole life as part of a big family group it was weird to suddenly be living with just one or two other people. It was like being an only child for a while.

Kenny lived close by so he started picking me up at 5:45 a.m. every morning for training. And when I say every morning I really do mean every single morning. Training with the Scots College boys was good because I got to be around players who were mostly at the same level as me. That meant we all improved together. But training with Kenny in the mornings was a whole different thing. He'd open up the Show Buildings at 6 a.m. every day and whoever was there would train with him.

You could have been literally anyone in Wellington and if you turned up at the Show Buildings at 6 a.m. you'd get a free training session with one of the best coaches in the country. That's what Kenny had been offering for years before I showed up. No one ever paid for those sessions, which seems incredible to me now.

Whenever it was particularly gross weather or cold, there would be fewer players, and there were a lot of mornings where it would be just Kenny and me. If there were tournaments coming up for school or rep teams, suddenly the place would fill up with everyone trying to get in some last-minute workouts. But no matter how many players showed up, I was always there and doing anything and everything Kenny told me to.

Our workouts were always simple. Ball handling, post moves, defense, and shooting. Youth basketball in New Zealand has a tendency to pigeonhole players in one position from a young age. If you're short, just work on your ball handling and shooting; if you're tall, just worry about rebounding and post moves. Kenny never believed in that. No matter who showed up to train, we all did the same drills. I'd be doing dribbling drills alongside some tiny girl point guard and then later she'd be at the next hoop working on the same post moves as me. Kenny only cared about taking care of the fundamentals. If players wanted to practice their dunk moves they could do that after training in their own time.

I noticed that whenever new faces showed up at morning trainings, they'd usually be really good at one or two drills and then really bad at another couple. And it would take them a while to even out their skillset (some never managed to) because it's hard to make yourself do the drills that you're bad at when you could just do the ones you're the best at. This wasn't a problem for me because I was fairly useless at everything when I met Kenny, so he had a blank canvas to work with. I suppose the thing that I had as my advantage was knowing how much I needed to work on and then actually being willing to do the work. I trusted that Kenny knew what he was doing so I followed him blindly. That's not something every athlete is lucky enough to have. A coach who you can truly trust will do right by you.

We started off right back at the beginning. Dribbling on the spot, dribbling left-handed, walking and dribbling, layups. Maybe if I was a more self-conscious person I wouldn't have wanted to train with Kenny and have people see me—a massive lanky guy who looked like he should be amazing at basketball— struggling with a dribbling drill that kids learn when they are seven. But the one thing that kept me going back was the progress I was making.

Starting from scratch meant the only way for me to go was up. And I gotta say, I moved pretty quickly. But even as I was progressing and moving on to more complex drills and workouts, Kenny kept me doing the fundamentals all the way through. I could dunk, but it was months before Kenny let me dunk during a drill. First, I had to be able to get the ball in the hoop every other way.

Four weeks after I moved in to Blossom's place, she told me that she had managed to get me a spot at Scots College. Moving to Wellington hadn't scared me. Waking up at 5:30 a.m. every morning to train was all good. But being told that I'd be going to Scots freaked me out.

Scots is a fancy, private, all boys Presbyterian school in Wellington. I'd seen the basketball guys come out of the changing room after trainings in their hard-out school uniforms with maroon blazers and ties. They looked like little businessmen on their way to the office to file some reports. The school buildings were even more intimidating. From what I'd seen while driving through to the gym, it was like some sort of brick castle. It didn't look like any school I'd seen. Although I hadn't seen much of Scots, I'd seen enough to know that I definitely didn't belong there. And that was confirmed when I turned up for my first day of school in almost two years.

Everyone stared at me. Everyone has always stared at me because of my height, but this time I knew it wasn't just about that. All the students were staring at me because they were scared. I looked like a murderer. I'd only just gotten into the habit of showering regularly thanks to Blossom getting on my back about it, but we hadn't progressed to grooming yet. So what the students—some as young as 11 years old—were seeing was a giant brown person with long, greasy hair and a dirty, wispy mustache. I didn't have a uniform yet because they were still trying to find one big enough for me. Instead I was wearing what I wore every day: basketball shorts, a probably unwashed T-shirt, and my orange basketball shoes that had nearly fallen apart. At least they were better than what I was walking around in when I first got to Wellington—old basketball shoes with the front half of the sole completely worn off so that I was pretty much walking in socks. When it rained I'd put my feet into plastic bread bags to try to stop my socks from getting wet. I could see why the other students didn't want to come near me. But luckily for everyone, I wanted to be there even less than they wanted me to be there.

I was taken to the full school assembly that day and introduced to everyone. I could see the teachers were even more put off than the kids. I found out later that some of them didn't think I'd last at the school beyond the end of the year. I would like to say that I never would have considered it, but, honestly, if they had said that to my face on that first day I probably would have agreed and left then and there. My first taste of discipline and structure at a school like Scots was when they said I couldn't wear the uniform and attend classes until I had "sorted out" my hair and the bum fluff on my upper lip. So Blossom took me to get my first ever professional haircut and I took a razor to my face, and suddenly I didn't look so borderline homeless anymore. They managed to find me a school uniform by the end of the first week and I went back for my first day of classes, more scared and resentful than I'd ever been.

Pat Fraser, from the basketball team, was told to be my buddy because everyone figured he'd met me and wouldn't be scared of me. But I'm pretty sure he was terrified for those first few days. It didn't help that I punched him in the stomach to test if we could be friends or not. I'm not a big talker and back then I could barely hold a conversation. For me, the only thing that mattered in a friend was whether or not they'd have my back if trouble started. And the only way to test this was to start trouble. While Pat was walking me around the school and answering my questions about everything, I punched him hard in the stomach. He turned around and gave me a mean uppercut right back, knocking the wind out of me. All right, I thought, this guy's cool. If someone tries to mess with me, he'll be right in there to take them on. I guess I was looking for someone to have my back like Sid had when I was younger. I found that in Pat, who has been my best friend ever since.

Having Pat as my friend helped a little with adjusting to the student culture, but that doesn't mean it was all smooth sailing. To put it bluntly, I was dumb. I could read, but that was about it. At 14 I had managed to avoid having to read and write my entire life, and suddenly there I was, attending one of the top academic schools in the country with a reading age of eight years old. On my second day I was taken to the school library to get a library card issued. I'd never had a library card before and already knew that I'd never use it, but it was compulsory so I signed up.

When I got to the library it was empty because everyone was

in class. It was quiet and had a lot of comfortable seating, which is hard to find at most schools. I knew on that first day that I would be spending a lot of time in the library over the next three years, to get away from all the hectic school stuff and clear my head.

At the start, I did virtually nothing besides eat a lot of food in the school cafeteria and try to avoid doing schoolwork. I figured that I didn't have to try that hard in the classroom as long as I was improving on the basketball court. I knew that at other schools rugby players got away with doing hardly any work because their rugby career didn't depend on it. I was still trying to get up to the national standard for reading and writing, but I dismissed it as unimportant because my improvements on the court were coming faster and faster.

From the beginning Ms. Glenda Parks, who was in charge of learning development and helped anyone who had fallen behind, became my mentor. A few months into that first year at Scots, I was sitting outside on a bench, wagging class and generally feeling sorry for myself. School was hard, and I couldn't fix it by going for a run and doing some push-ups. Basketball was at least distracting me from the fact that I was alone in a new city and without my dad, but at Scots I felt alienated.

I didn't notice Ms. Parks until she sat down right beside me and asked what was wrong. I mumbled the usual moanings of teenagers until she cut me off. "Steven," she said, making me look right at her. "How badly do you want this?" The only other person to ask me that was Kenny, and answering him was easy because I was more than ready to commit to basketball every day. But when Ms. Parks asked me, I realized that committing to basketball also meant committing to school, a place I tried to avoid at all costs. "I want it bad," I said. She nodded and replied, "Well, then this is something we're just going to have to do." It didn't flick a switch and make me suddenly want to learn, but it stopped me from actively avoiding learning, and that's saying a lot.

While I was still working every morning with Kenny, he had me train with the Wellington rep team that he was coaching. They were good. Really good. That year they had underperformed at the Under 17 National Championships and were already training for the next year's tournament to redeem themselves. Rep basketball begins with the under 13 age group, so kids generally start playing the best players in their age group from around the country when they are 11 years old. By the time they get to be 15, everyone knows which are the teams to beat and which players are the stars.

This particular Wellington team had been the team to beat for a few years already. They didn't necessarily need a new recruit, but they got me anyway. There was never a proper introduction. There never seemed to be any formal introductions in the Wellington basketball community. Hanging out at the Show Buildings every morning for three months meant that I had seen almost all of the under 17 players come in for a morning workout at least once, though never as a full team.

By the time I joined one of their team trainings with Kenny, I'd gotten used to working out on my own. Suddenly, I was put into a team where the guys had played together and against each other for five years. It was Scots College all over again. But when it came to basketball I had already worked out what I really wanted and set myself a daunting goal: scoring a college scholarship in the United States. I knew that playing well in that team was crucial for my ongoing improvement and my plan for the rest of my life.

I truly didn't care if everyone in the team hated me, so long as I got to go up against the best school-aged players in the country and prove my worth on the court. Thankfully, I never had to worry about that because the Wellington rep team became my family and my teammates became brothers for life. Chris McIntyre, the tall guy who had been mean to me at the training camp earlier in the year, was on the team and once again paired up with me. Except this time we were on the same team and I was able to learn from him instead of being outsmarted. Chris was, and is, a genius. All the guys in our team were awesome at basketball, but none of us were that great in the classroom except for Chris and Stanley, one of the shooting guards. Chris's brain was like a computer. We started calling him Google because he knew the answer to every single question we asked. I thought maybe he was just smart compared to me, which wasn't hard, but it turns out he's smart compared to everyone. He's at Oxford now on a Rhodes Scholarship, in case you needed proof.

Although we were complete opposites, Chris and I formed a friendship based on our completely different strengths. Chris was glad to have me join the team so that he had help getting the boards and wasn't the only big guy in the team. He was tall, but he wasn't huge, so he preferred to play farther out, sometimes even on the perimeter. With me there as a giant inside presence, Chris got to have more fun with taking longer shots.

And I enjoyed having Chris around because I like to surround myself with people who are smarter than me.

Even though I didn't have the basketball knowledge other guys had built up, I made the team and was put in the starting five. There were no complaints about some new guy swooping in and taking someone's spot because everyone already knew that winning as a team mattered more than personal pride and ego. The team was a well-oiled machine, thanks in large part to Kenny as coach and Debbie Webb, the manager. Debbie was famous in the Wellington basketball community. She had managed almost all of Kenny's teams, first when her son Tom was playing and then when her son Joseph played, who was the same age as me and a point guard.

Most young rep teams will have a coach and an assistant coach who could act as manager. Kenny didn't need any help coaching so Debbie was full-time manager and Mum to all us boys. It was incredible. She always had our tournament weeks plotted out right down to the minute and organized a heap of fundraisers so we wouldn't have to pay much for fees, if anything at all. Debbie wasn't afraid to tell us off if we misbehaved, and everyone treated her with the same respect they'd treat their own mum with. I considered Debbie to be a maternal figure for me even before she took me into her home as part of her family.

Things had been humming along nicely at Blossom's place, where we'd sorted out a routine between us. But before the end of that first year, Blossom was a having a hard time sourcing enough income and couldn't afford to have me stay anymore. I didn't hold it against her at all. How could I when she'd done so much for me already? And even though I knew that this whole basketball thing was what I wanted to do and what I *should* do,

I missed Rotorua and being around my family. So I went home. I packed up my bag of clothes and took a bus back to Rotorua, where I guess we all assumed I'd go back to what I was doing six months earlier—nothing.

But back in Wellington, Kenny wasn't ready to let his new project slip away that easily. He talked to Debbie and asked if she and her husband, Chris, would be willing to let me stay with them until Blossom got back on her feet. Kenny knew that the Webbs lived in a big house on a lifestyle block on the fringes of the city, and he also knew that they lived and breathed Wellington basketball. As unco as I was, I would be really helpful on that Wellington team. Kenny knew that Debbie was his best shot at getting me back to training in Wellington. Without hesitating, or even asking how long I would be staying, Debbie said, "Yes, absolutely," and I'll always love her for that.

Living with the Webbs was a surreal experience for me. They were like the families you see in advertisements on TV. It was just Debbie and Chris, their son Joseph, and me living there. They had the nicest home I had ever lived in and a big section of land with a few animals on it. It wasn't a farm like the ones Mohi worked on, but it was the closest you could get to farm life while still living near the city.

Although Joseph and I shared a room, we had the whole downstairs to ourselves with its own bathroom and lounge. Joseph had been coming to morning trainings most days and as soon as I moved in he started coming every single day too. After all, we were sharing a room, so it's not like he could just sleep in while his teammate went off to train at the crack of dawn.

Debbie and Chris would make bacon and egg–filled English muffins and wrap them in tinfoil for us to eat after training, and I would drink all the milk in their fridge. I'd say I drank at least a liter a day: regular milk, chocolate milk, banana milk.... That was my hydration throughout the day. I know now that milk is expensive, but the Webbs never mentioned anything; they just always had the fridge stocked and told me not to hold back. Scots College was providing lunch for me, so the Webbs only had to give me breakfast and dinner, but I still ate more than the average person.

Every morning the whole household would be up by 5:30 a.m. and ready to go. I'm not a morning person at all, but it's hard to stay in bed when everyone around you is up and moving. Joseph and I would be dropped off at the Show Buildings at 6 a.m., train for two hours with Kenny, get showered, then go to school. Joseph went to Wellington College, which was just down the road, but Scots College was miles away so Kenny would drop me off. After school I would catch the school bus to the train station to meet Joseph and we'd get the train home together.

Debbie ran a tight ship when she managed her teams and she ran a tight ship at home, which was ideal for me. Everyone had a routine and mine slotted in alongside Joseph's nicely. When he did his homework, I did my homework, or at least I tried to. Then we'd have a break and play table tennis or go outside to shoot on their hoop. They had a whole half-court set up with a proper hoop, not one of those cheap ones you get for $50. I figured it would be strong, but I forgot to factor in that it had been outside in the wind and rain for months. I told Joseph to watch me while I ran up, gripped the ball in both hands and tried to dunk it how I'd seen players do on TV. The hoop broke clean off the backboard and I landed on the ground still holding it. They never did replace that hoop.

I'd like to think I made up for breaking the Webbs' hoop by helping out on their lifestyle block. They only had about 30 lambs and a few cattle, but it still needed work, and over the course of a few weekends, Chris, Joseph, and I put up a new fence running down their hilly section. I knew all about fences. Fences were my thing. So when it came time to get things set up and in place, I was there in my Swanndri and carrying fence posts like it was a paid gig. Doing some work on their section wasn't quite the full Mohi farm experience, but it helped to ease a bit of the homesickness I would occasionally feel. As much as I enjoyed seeing myself improve in the gym, being virtually a full-time athlete at 15 years old can get draining. Instead of doing nothing to unwind, I preferred doing something productive, like building a fence. Or breaking a hoop.

I lived with the Webbs for almost six months. There's no way they anticipated that I would be staying for that long when Kenny first pitched the idea to them, and yet I never heard them grumble. They didn't even get that mad when I accidentally kicked a hole in their wall while trying to dance.

When Blossom got sorted I started staying with her again for a few days a week and eventually moved back in with her full-time because it was hard to argue with the convenience. She lived close to Scots College and to Kenny, who could drive me to and from trainings when Blossom was at work. I would do whatever it took to achieve my goal of a scholarship and playing professional basketball, and I think everyone involved—me,

Kenny, Blossom, the Webbs—knew that living with Blossom was the right thing for me.

Moving back in with Blossom didn't mean life just went back to how it was before I'd left. It had been six months and she'd kept in contact with Kenny to follow my progress on the court. When I settled back in with Blossom, she announced that it was time for me to hit the gym. I thought I already was hitting the gym, but she insisted I needed to build up my strength with weights in an actual gym. Blossom was a personal trainer at Les Mills, so she was able to get me in there to work out if I wanted. Like everything else, I didn't actually know what I wanted, but I did know that Blossom knew what she was doing, so I trusted her.

Yet another training session was added to my daily routine. On top of the morning trainings and the after-school and social games at night, I did a workout with Blossom at Les Mills, usually right after school and before the night game. Sometimes I'd just join in on a spin class, but other times Blossom would take me through a personalized workout. I've always been naturally strong, or at least proportionally strong, but I was never a force to be reckoned with. Blossom had talked to Kenny and knew that the goal wasn't for me to get muscly, it was for me to be stronger overall, especially in my core.

Most of the time I was the only kid in the gym because gym memberships are expensive. I didn't know this at the time and just thought other kids were too busy socializing to bother. I thought a personal coach and personal trainer were what every athletic kid could have if they wanted it. I've since realized that having someone willing to train you one-on-one for free in the basketball gym, and then *another* person to work with you every day in the weight room, is bloody rare. Kenny and Blossom wouldn't have pushed me so hard for so long if I had turned out to be lazy and not committed to the goal, but not everyone has people in their life like that.

Our Wellington rep team was good because we had a stacked bench. New Zealand is small and basketball isn't the main sport, so even good rep teams will have a few players who don't contribute much. We had a full roster, where everyone was crucial to the team and had a role to play. That was Kenny putting together a championship-caliber team from the very beginning, but we were also good because we trained harder and better than everyone else. Kenny has always said that if he could get New Zealand athletes to train like American athletes, we'd have a lot more players in the NBA and the WNBA.

When I first went to Kenny, I was so naive and unaccustomed to the training methods for most young basketballers in New Zealand that he was able to train me like an American—every day, twice a day, a full-time commitment. And when he coached a Wellington rep team, he demanded that same commitment. Our team always trained more than any other Wellington team. The open morning trainings became just another team training for us. Even though they weren't compulsory, almost everyone showed up, because if you didn't, you'd be behind on the plays at the next official team training.

The team was a playoff team with a new asset (me) and we seemed unstoppable before we'd even played a proper game. Then we took the court for our first game at the regional tournament— and promptly lost.

6.

NATIONAL CHAMPIONS

I wish I didn't have to use this comparison, but it's the only one that works. Our Wellington team was the Golden State Warriors of New Zealand basketball. Our team was *stacked*, and everyone knew it.

Every year there are tournaments for each age group, under 13, under 15, under 17, right up to under 23. At the start of winter there are four regional tournaments. The top four finishers from each region qualify for the National Championships, which are held a few months later over one week. The idea is that the semifinals at Nationals would be made up of regional tournament winners. That's the idea anyway.

We were in region three, which is basically just the wider Wellington region and a few extras like Hawke's Bay, New Plymouth, and Palmerston North. We knew going in that Hawke's Bay would be our biggest regional rivals, but we had the same defensive approach to them as to every other team—let them shoot and crash the boards. It's rare for a young team to have a high overall field goal percentage so we knew that as long as we got all the rebounds and ran our offense, we'd be fine.

What we didn't count on was for every Hawke's Bay player to shoot the lights out in our game. Their main weapon was a tall white guy who was playing as a four man but who could shoot threes all day. I mention he's white because in New Zealand there aren't a whole lot of standout white players. National tournaments, especially the girls' ones, are overwhelmingly made up of Māori or Pacific Islanders, and the Hawke's Bay team was no different. But this one guy must have shot 80 percent from the perimeter and we couldn't do anything to stop him. It was a much-needed wake-up call.

Losing at Regionals is a sign that you will struggle to make the top four at Nationals. We were planning to take out the whole championship but couldn't even win the first game at our local tournament. After the loss, Kenny sat us down for a team debrief and we realized that even stacked teams can lose when they come up against a team that gels on the night. On one hand, there's not a lot you can do when a guy is hot and can't seem to miss, but we knew we needed to pay Hawke's Bay more respect next time around. Victor, the guy I had blocked at my very first training camp and who was now a small forward, called out Joseph and a couple of other guys for not hustling enough. "Every loose ball should be ours," he said, "but you guys aren't scrambling." It must have got into Joseph's head because the next game he was diving all over the floor like someone was dropping money.

We met Hawke's Bay again in the final at the end of the week.

This time we went in with a chip on our shoulder and ended up winning comfortably.

A few months later at Nationals we progressed steadily through pool play and into the finals without any real challenges. After a tense final (are they ever not tense?) we were the Under 17 National Champions. It was the perfect reward for every early-morning and late-night scrimmage we'd gone through. I was named Most Valuable Player at the tournament, which was a genuine surprise because I'd always thought MVP went to a standout player on a team. I considered myself purely a role player in our team, but I guess when you're 6'9", you have to be pretty useless to not have a good-looking stat sheet by the end of a weeklong tournament.

What mattered more to me about winning the championship and being MVP was that it validated all the work I was putting in. I hope that if we'd come in ninth at that tournament and I didn't play that well I would have still pursued a life in basketball, but I can't say for sure. I'm just lucky I never had to find out. My first full year of training with Kenny and I was a national champion and tournament MVP. It was about as much proof of progress as I could have hoped for, and it told me that I was on the right track and surrounded by the right people.

After Nationals the rest of the guys took a break from training together to concentrate on their various school teams, as the season was still ongoing. I had no time to rest. If anything, I came back from Nationals wanting to work even harder so that by the next year I could blow everyone out of the water.

Everyone else in the team went to public schools and played in the top basketball grade, while I was two grades down playing against some quite shambolic teams because I was at a private school that just didn't have the same pool of basketball talent. It was good for me, though, because it forced me to develop some leadership skills. Instead of being able to just work on my own game and let everyone else around me work on theirs, I suddenly had so-called expertise that my Scots teammates lacked. Having to teach a drill or technique to someone else is honestly the best way to fully understand it yourself. Playing for a not so great school team was a blessing in disguise because it broke up my season and offered some variety in the style of play I was facing.

For everyone in that Wellington team, though, winning Nationals every year was the number-one priority, no exceptions. Because of how the age groups are set up—under 15, under 17, under 19, and under 21—every second year it's common to have a different team. Most of us were born in the same year so we got to stay together in the same rep team for four years. After winning Nationals in 2009, we knew we had to win every tournament now. And that's exactly what we did.

From 2009 to 2012, we lost only one game, against Hawke's Bay in that first regional tournament. From there on we were undefeated and ended up with four national titles, plus I walked away with four MVP trophies. The bond that we had as a team was the strongest I've had with any team, including the Thunder.

Half of us came from families without money, which meant we fundraised a lot to pay for travel costs and tournament fees. Debbie soon had a list of go-to businesses who would effectively hire the whole team to work an event. She started working with Bernice, another team mum, and together they became the ultimate managing duo. We marshaled cycling events, ran stalls on the weekends, and held car washes and auctions right throughout the year so that once the tournaments came around we had no costs. It was work, but it never felt like it because we were hanging out with our mates off the court. It didn't matter if you could afford to pay the fees without fundraising; every single player worked those weekends to bring the costs down for their teammates who had less. No matter how good a team is on the court, if they can't work together and get along off the court, there's going to be problems.

Only now when I stop to think about it do I realize that there were probably times when our fundraising didn't cover all the costs of a tournament, particularly if it required a flight to get there. But even though I had no money, I never felt as if I was in danger of not being able to go. The only explanation for this is that if there were any extra expenses, Kenny, Blossom, Bernice, or the Webbs looked after them without telling me. I was a big part of the team so it makes sense they would want me at the tournaments, but at the same time, quietly paying for someone else's kid to play basketball is just one of the many things that people did to help me get to the NBA. I've never brought it up with Debbie or Bernice, because I know they would either deny it or avoid the question. It was just something people did and didn't need to have discussed. I may have had nothing to my name, but I was always provided for by others, and then some.

The tournaments were always the highlights of the year. If you're reading this and you have kids, please sign them up to play at least one team sport. Spending a week living with friends who shared a common passion and goal was crucial to my development, both as a player and as an empathetic person.

Traveling to tournaments in New Zealand meant squashing into vans and driving up to 12 hours to get to the host city. Once there, accommodation was either a motel or a holiday park and campground. Some teams would stay on marae to save money, which meant everyone slept in sleeping bags on rows of mattresses on the floor. It was virtually impossible to have time alone, but no one really wanted it, because why would you wander off by yourself during a weeklong sleepover with your friends?

Our team went through our awkward teenage years together, which meant there was a lot of dick swinging and dick measuring (literally), but it was also the first time I had close friends to talk to about things I was too scared or embarrassed to ask the adults in my life. When you're a kid and you have nothing, your only assets are your relationships. Through Wellington basketball I was made rich with friends who will always be my brothers, even though we don't see much of each other these days. We had each other's backs on and off the court.

The best example of this was when we were out of town for a tournament and a group of us walked by a house where some Mongrel Mob gang members were having a party. They yelled something at us that I couldn't hear but which Victor could. Victor yelled back at them and next thing I knew they were marching onto the street looking like they were going to smash all of us. When they got closer I think they realized how big Chris and I were so they stopped, spat at us, and went back to their drinking. If they'd wanted to fight they would have nailed the lot of us, and I would have been the first to go down. I stood there, scared, but knowing that none of the boys would run away, because you never leave your teammate, whether you're on the court or off. That stays with me, as strong as ever, to this day.

More than titles, more than money, what really counts is the confidence you have in your teammates, and that they have in you.

7.

MAKE OR BREAK

I like being the underdog because the only way is up. I relish people doubting me because being able to prove them wrong is so damn satisfying. Luckily for me, there were plenty of people to prove wrong in 2010 and 2011, the busiest, most stressful years of my life. And before you mutter *"so far,"* I honestly don't think I will experience another period that is as busy and important as those two years were for me. If school and sport count as work—and I believe they do—then I was working 16-hour days. With at least two trainings a day and games every second day on top of school and homework, I didn't have time for anything else.

At the end of 2010 I went along to a Junior Tall Blacks training camp because Kenny was the coach and I was able to go without paying the fee. That's right, in New Zealand promising young basketballers have to pay to trial for national teams. Kenny had invited the coach from the University of Pittsburgh, Jamie Dixon, to watch and scout for potential recruits for his NCAA Division I side. I performed well at the camp and Jamie was interested right off the bat. We had a talk and arranged for him to come and see me train a bit more in 2011. But he made it clear on that first visit that he wanted me to go to Pitt on a scholarship.

I never ended up playing for Kenny's Junior Tall Blacks team. I was obviously good enough—a national MVP should be able to make the junior national team—but I couldn't afford it. To represent New Zealand as a young athlete costs a lot of money, not just in basketball but in all sports. Being selected for an age-group national side to play in an international tournament would cost each player thousands of dollars. I knew of players who went on every trip, at least once a year, because their parents could easily afford to pay for each tournament. But there were a lot of players, most of them brown, some of them the best in the country, who never once represented New Zealand because they couldn't afford to trial, let alone to fly overseas. I hate to think how many guys I played with who could have had careers in basketball if they'd just been given more help (like I was) when they were younger.

While I didn't mind the hours of training and gym workouts, I was finding it harder and harder to be enthusiastic about schoolwork. I couldn't figure out why I had to spend at least six hours a day doing things that wouldn't matter if I succeeded in becoming a professional basketball player. I want everything I do to be in pursuit of a greater goal and, by the start of my final year at Scots, I wasn't seeing how school was helping me reach my goal.

But while the end goal was never to get a scholarship, it was a required step in continuing to improve my game, and therefore schoolwork was a vital area that I was neglecting. That is, until Blossom sat me down and gave it to me straight. Without good grades, I wouldn't get a scholarship. Without a scholarship I wouldn't get to America. And if I didn't get to America, there wasn't much chance of me getting to the NBA. That was all it took. Just a no-nonsense explanation of *why* I needed to succeed in school and my attitude changed completely.

We found out which requirements I'd need in order to study at a Division I college in America and realized that I was taking all the wrong subjects at school. In my first full year at Scots, I didn't progress much in the classroom. Where I did progress was in catching up socially and integrating into the school community. So, to no one's surprise, my grades weren't very good that year. A lot of papers I didn't achieve and the ones I did were the unit standards, which were usually easier to pass. In 2010 I was a Year 12 student and started to be more comfortable in the classroom, but I still struggled a lot, especially with written subjects like English. So I took all the classes that students take when they know they're not good in the classroom, like physical education, computing, and tech.

It soon became clear that I couldn't keep taking the subjects I wanted and be accepted into a Division I college. For the first time in my life I started having regrets. Why hadn't I worked harder when I first got to Scots? Why had I never gone to school in Rotorua? Why had I acted like school wasn't as important as basketball?

The principal at Scots spoke to one of the English teachers, Ms. Milne, and asked if she would tutor me to get my grades up.

She said yes (I'm starting to wonder if anyone ever refused to help me) and would come to meet me every study period for an extra lesson.

It wasn't easy. I might have never missed a training and always put in 100 percent on the court, but the same could not be said for my work in the classroom. Ms. Milne, Ms. Parks, and Ms. Esterman, the librarian, were my three school mums and they had their work cut out for them. To get my literacy credits I had to complete a reading log, which meant I had to start reading.

Two years earlier I had met Ms. Esterman in the library and she had asked me what books I liked to read. I said, *"Where's Wally?"* That's where my interest in reading was at. She found a *Where's Wally?* book from the primary school library and we went through it together before she gently suggested that I try out a short novel. From there it was very slow but steady progress until in 2011 she handed me *Catch Me If You Can*, a story of a con artist, made famous by its movie version featuring Leonardo DiCaprio. I carried that book around with me everywhere. But I hardly read it. Ms. Milne would make jokes about me always having that book in my hand; I had every intention of reading it, but most of the time I'd get through half a page then get distracted by something more interesting, for example, a tumbleweed blowing across the rugby field. Even the title *Catch Me If You Can* became a joke among the teachers, who had to chase me around the school trying to get me to complete their assignments. It wasn't that I didn't take schoolwork seriously, it was just so much harder for me to work with my brain than with my body.

I loved math and classics. Math, because everything is either right or wrong, and once I understood a formula I could sit all day solving problems and getting a kick out of each correct answer. Classics I loved because of the stories. The best mark I ever got in school (besides the PE physical that I aced) was a merit in a level 2 classics assignment. The learning material was pretty much the same as all the other assignments that year, but the difference was that we had to deliver our work as a seminar. I knew what story I wanted to teach the class about, so I went up in front of them and told it. I spoke for 15 minutes with no notes, no cue cards, nothing. My issue was never that I didn't understand ideas and concepts, it was that I couldn't write them down.

When the principal came into the common room the next week and announced that Steven Adams, the guy who could barely read when he started at Scots, had gotten a merit for his classics seminar, I'd never been more proud. All my mates were shocked, and I played it off as if I just got lucky, but in my mind I was strutting around like a peacock.

Ms. Milne knew that I worked better verbally, so we went through most of our tutoring sessions having conversations about things I was reading, rather than her making me write down a bunch of answers. I requested a reader–writer for exams, someone who sits with you and writes out your words for you. Some people might consider having a reader–writer to be a bit embarrassing or something to be ashamed of, but I didn't hesitate in asking. When there was a mix-up and one wasn't there for an exam, I didn't start until she arrived.

I am proud of my strengths, but I am also aware of my weaknesses. I wasn't actually dumb—I understood the concepts and knew what to say—but barely going to school until I was 14 meant my writing was a hindrance in timed assessments. I think that if you have something you're not confident with, own it and accept the extra assistance when it's available. If I had refused to be humbled by all those who could help me, I'd still be sleeping on a mattress in Rotorua.

Ms. Milne wasn't just my tutor during her breaks and after school, she also played the role of part-time driver. If we had a lesson after school and I needed to get to the gym to meet Blossom, which was every day, I'd wait by Ms. Milne's car and ask if she would be going through town on her way home. She almost always was—or at least that's what she said. She would drive me into town in her tiny RAV4 with no leg room and drop me off at the gym. I've never been one to let pride get in the way of a free ride.

To everyone's surprise but my own, spending so much more time at school didn't take anything away from my basketball. I was still training every morning with Kenny, although my new training buddy was a guard called Jah Wee, who had the biggest hops of anyone I'd met but wanted to work on his court reading. He played in the Wellington rep team and lived not far from Blossom and Kenny.

Kenny would be outside Jah Wee's house at 5:20 a.m. each morning and if he wasn't waiting outside, Kenny would drive away. For two years, Jah Wee was always waiting outside. Then they would come by Blossom's house to pick me up and I would never be outside, so Jah Wee would have to come inside and get me. I can't count the number of times I woke up to Jah Wee standing over me, telling me to hurry up.

As I started to get some media attention later that year, reporters loved to mention that I would have to be up and standing outside by 5:30 a.m. every morning. In reality I was given a lot of passes from Kenny, and Jah Wee was the only one who risked missing a training by sleeping in because no one was going to go inside to wake him up. It wasn't that I didn't want to train; I've just never been a morning person. One of the best things about playing basketball for a living now is that I never have to wake up at 5 a.m. I start work at 9 a.m. like a normal person.

During one training, Kenny casually mentioned that he had been speaking to Pero Cameron, a former Tall Black and current coach of the Wellington Saints, the city's team in the National Basketball League. Cameron apparently wanted me to play for his team in the 2011 season.

Some of us in the Wellington rep team had been training occasionally with the Saints, but I thought it was just to get in some extra hours in the gym, not to actually play for them. The training had been a massive step up and improved my game heaps in a short time as a result of matching up against much stronger and more experienced players. The Saints had guys like Nick Horvath and Kareem Johnson in their squad, who had both played basketball in America. Nick had won an NCAA Division I title playing for Duke University and he had also played for the Los Angeles Lakers and Minnesota Timberwolves in their Summer League teams. Guarding Nick and Kareem quickly made me realize that to play in the NBA you have to be at a whole other level of toughness because even in practice those guys would throw you all over the court.

My first game playing for the Saints was at TSB Arena in Wellington, our home court. I was so nervous before the game that I threw up. Heaps of my mates from Scots College were there as well as a whole bunch of teachers. I'd never had that many people come to a game just to see me play and that didn't exactly help with my nerves.

I have never been as anxious about a game of basketball as I was for that first Saints game. Not even playing my first game in the NBA compares. I don't remember who we played, but we won, and I didn't make a fool of myself—and that was all that mattered to me. As the season went on, I started to come off the bench earlier and got more minutes, which grew my confidence and let me finish the season with some really strong games behind me. It was during this season that I finally grew confident enough to dunk on people, not just around them.

We won the championship that year, winning the final against, of all teams, Hawke's Bay, and continuing my unbeaten streak with Wellington basketball teams. I was named Rookie of the Year. I got to line up against the best players in the country, and the Saints got a big man for free because if they had paid me I would no longer be an amateur and would have been ineligible to play college basketball in the United States. Kenny was really careful about that. He'd known some guys who didn't understand the rules and had accepted payment for playing in a random tournament, and then lost their scholarships.

University of Pittsburgh had committed to giving me a full scholarship the following year and I certainly wasn't about to put that in jeopardy. The Pittsburgh coach Jamie Dixon had visited New Zealand again after the Junior Tall Blacks camp and had come to a game that our Wellington rep team was playing against Kapiti to warm up for Nationals. Kapiti has never been a strong basketball unit so there wasn't much to see, which is lucky because, thanks to the many weird NCAA recruiting rules, Jamie had to stand outside the whole game. If he'd come inside, though, he would have seen me shattering the Kapiti College backboard and breaking their hoop. I'm not sure if that would have helped or hurt my chances, now that I think about it. Either way, Coach Dixon soon confirmed my scholarship offer.

I never considered other colleges in America besides Pittsburgh because there weren't any to consider. Back then, to get a scholarship you needed a connection to a college and the only one we had was Jamie, who had played basketball with Kenny decades earlier. These days, there are more and more college scouts coming to watch the New Zealand Secondary Schools National Championships every year, which is incredible to see because it gives players options to find a U.S. college that best fits them as a player and as a student. I went to Pitt because they were the first to ask.

In August 2011, I attended the adidas Nations tournament in Los Angeles for the second time. I had gone the year before when it was held in Chicago and while I thought I did okay, I definitely didn't blow anyone away. The best part of it was getting a whole bunch of free adidas gear. I could finally stop wearing the same three T-shirts everywhere and I didn't have to buy any new socks for years. But in 2011 I had made huge improvements, I had upped my training to twice a day during the school term and four times a day in the holidays, and I was feeling fitter than ever after my season with the Saints. The tournament was a massive success. I played with Team Asia, and although we lost all our games we were at least competitive. I ended up averaging 22 points, 16 rebounds, and two assists over four games. They were my impressive stats.

My unimpressive stats were the few media interviews I did. I can't bear to watch any of those old interviews now because I sound completely lost. During one, the poor interviewer was getting absolutely nothing from me, like even shorter answers than Russell Westbrook gives these days. After a few minutes trying to get more than two-word answers, he asked, "What are your strengths and weaknesses?" I looked at him for a while, thought about it, and managed to come up with "I dunno, just...running." I seriously listed running as a strength. Wanna know what my second strength was? Playing. I nearly cry thinking about how bad I was at answering questions back then. Like anything, it's a skill and one I clearly hadn't learned at that point. Thankfully, players aren't recruited solely on how well they can string a sentence together or there would be a lot fewer players in the NBA right now.

I heard later that what impressed the coaches and reporters wasn't that I was scoring lots of points, but that I was able to score points *and* defend well against the big names in my recruiting class, the biggest being Kaleb Tarczewski, another 7-foot center. Kaleb's name had been floating around the tournament as one to watch, but I knew if I just played my own game and hustled on defense, I wouldn't have any trouble matching up against him. I came away with 20 points, 24 rebounds, and four assists. Kaleb had 10 points and four rebounds.

To be honest, I was used to this happening. Even in New Zealand I was often considered an underdog in match-ups with big guys whose names had been thrown around the circuit well before I'd even started playing. But I always managed to outplay them.

The first examples were two North Shore players, Isaac Fotu and Rob Loe. I like both those guys and they are great players, but the first time I played them at under 19s, everyone expected me to be outclassed by their experience. Instead I was able to outhustle and outmuscle both players on the way to another New Zealand national championship.

During my final year of school, I really started to get the media's attention. Being 7 feet tall was enough to make it into the local newspaper every once in a while, but after I signed on to the Saints, I started to get some real coverage. And New Zealand quickly displayed its usual tall poppy syndrome. Yes, most of the attention was good and supportive, but there were still a lot of people saying that I only got picked because I was tall or—and this was a real weird one—because I was Valerie Adams's brother. I knew how good I was so it didn't bother me too much, but it's hard to completely ignore comments like that, especially as a teenager.

As I started to play more for the Saints and to show my worth, the comments didn't go away, they just morphed into new insults. Since they couldn't say that I wasn't good enough for the Saints, they started saying that the NBL itself wasn't that great and once I got to America I'd soon learn that I didn't have what it takes to play Division I ball. I don't know what it is with some New Zealanders, but they really take the notion of being "humble" seriously. So seriously that they'll do their best to humble you if they think you're not doing it for yourself. Did people want me to say that I didn't think I could make the NBA or succeed in basketball? Did they want me to act surprised that recruiters were saying I was good? I didn't train every morning for four years to not be good or to pretend that I just got lucky.

The other thing that I wasn't prepared for were the assumptions about my family and my childhood. I'd deliberately been vague about my background because I preferred to keep some things private, and I didn't want to suddenly have my family in the papers. Somehow, in doing that, I got an even worse outcome. One mention by me of not going to school and suddenly I was "living on the streets." A random anecdote about being friends with someone whose dad was in the Mongrel Mob and soon I was reading about how I was on the verge of joining a gang. That one made me laugh because if I'd even tried to get in with a gang my sister Viv would have yanked me right back out again. Even though I thought these stretched truths were funny, I knew it was hurtful to my siblings who had looked out for me and were now being painted as absent or even neglectful guardians. No one ever mentioned my mum, even though she was around, which I'm sure she didn't appreciate.

The family talked with Val about how we should deal with these stories as she was the only one with media experience, and she said the best thing was to say nothing. So that's exactly what I did. I said nothing and watched as Steven Adams became an orphaned kid living on the streets, stealing and getting into fights, and about to join a gang before he was plucked from the gutter and brought to Wellington.

By the end of 2011 and my years at Scots College I had comfortably passed all the exams required for entry to college in the U.S. It meant I wouldn't have to go to summer school at Pittsburgh or take a bridging academic course to qualify for my scholarship. Unfortunately, because so many players end up having to delay their college careers as their grades are unsatisfactory, Pitt had taken the safe route and enrolled me into Notre Dame Preparatory School in Massachusetts. Even though I didn't need to go there, they kept me enrolled anyway so that I could get used to the American style of basketball. I figured that was probably a good idea, but it meant having to leave for the U.S. almost as soon as the New Zealand school year finished instead of having a break to spend time with friends and family.

Once again, I shrugged it off, knowing that if I let myself dwell on it for too long it would be no good for my game and my mental wellbeing. Besides, Notre Dame sounded like a cool place to learn the ropes of American basketball, and I couldn't wait for the step up in intensity.

While I had been focusing on my basketball I still tried to play other sports as much as possible. Experts used to say that kids had to choose their one sport as early as they could and stick to it. But my time spent playing rugby and doing athletics was only ever beneficial to my basketball. So while I was training hard out with Kenny I was also learning how to throw the shot put.

Every year, schools around New Zealand have athletics days

to pick a team to compete in local, then regional, then national meets. I won the shot-put event at Scots College because I was the tallest and no one else bothered with shot put. It's simple math; I had the better angles. Then I won the Wellington and the regional competitions and started to think maybe I was actually the man at shot put as well as basketball. It wasn't a completely ridiculous idea, as I at least had the genes for it. By then, Val was an Olympic gold medalist, winning at Beijing in 2008, and she would go on to win gold at the 2012 Olympics in London too.

The Wellington throws master, Shaka Sola, who represented Samoa in discus and shot put, had seen me throw at the regional meet and told me I should head to the athletics stadium that weekend to have a session with him. I didn't have any basketball on so I went along and soon figured out that he was the Kenny McFadden of throwing events. We went through some basic technical drills and I had improved my throw by the end of that first session. The thrill of such an immediate result got me hooked and I trained with Shaka every weekend for three months until the National Secondary Schools Athletics Championships.

I could see straight away why people get into individual sports like track and field. For someone who lives off seeing results, each increase to my PB was a new high. Basketball let me see improvements on the court as well, but with something like shot put, the evidence was right there in the measurements, and I became addicted to seeing that number go up.

Even though I'd only been training for a few months, my naturally competitive nature meant that I went into the national meet fully expecting to win. When I began training with Shaka,

I was throwing around 11 or 12 meters. By the time Nationals came around, I was throwing 15 meters and feeling confident.

What I had failed to notice were the occasional news stories about a guy called Jacko Gill who had set a junior world record at the age of 14 and won gold at the World Junior Championships. I showed up at the meet and went through the warm-ups with all the other part-time throwers while Jacko sat stretching on the side. He didn't look very big and was certainly not as tall as me. Then he got up for his one warm-up throw and heaved it close to 20 meters. "Man, what a dick," I thought. "At least pretend that you're trying." I finished up in fourth place and decided to end my athletics career then and there. I knew if I kept training I could add a few more meters to my throw and maybe even get somewhere close to Jacko's distances, but sometimes seeing someone excelling in their passion is enough to convince you to stick to yours.

At the end of my time at Scots College I was asked by the principal if I would be willing to make a speech to the entire school about what I hoped to be up to in years to come. Scholarships to American colleges were rare even then and I knew the school was proud of me for getting through my years at Scots and achieving academically. I hesitated for a couple of reasons, the main one being that I'd never spoken in front of a crowd before. I had gotten comfortable doing oral assignments in front of a class or a couple of teachers, but hundreds of students was a whole other deal.

I burst into Ms. Parks's office and told her I wasn't doing it. She had no idea what I was talking about as I ranted about why I couldn't possibly speak in front of the whole school and why everyone would think I was dumb. She didn't say anything. She just looked at me and I knew I had to do it. People had started to follow my story by then and I'd noticed some of the younger kids at the school seemed to look up to me, in every sense. It was the least I could do for a school that had taken a chance on a scruffy kid and helped him reach his goals. I worked on that speech with Blossom, I worked on that speech with Ms. Parks, I worked on that speech with my friends. I worked on that speech more than I had worked on any assignment or exam in all my time at school.

I included a little bit about my childhood—a topic I had staunchly avoided until then. I told them how I hated all of them when I first started at Scots and they laughed, maybe thinking I was joking. But I also spoke of how going to Scots had made me realize the importance of an education and that no matter what happened to my body, I'd always have the things I learned in the classroom. I spoke well. I was no Barack Obama, but I managed to get through it without any major fails and I got a huge round of applause. When I looked around at everyone I saw that a lot of the teachers were crying, particularly my three school mums. That's when I knew I'd done a good job. You know you've done well on the basketball court if your team wins and you contribute. But you know you've done a good job in delivering a speech if you make people cry.

It took three and a half years at a very expensive private school for me to realize the importance of an education. When I walked into Scots College I hated everything about it and I only wanted to be playing basketball. When I walked out of Scots College for the last time as a student, I knew that playing basketball wouldn't be possible without an education, and learning would still be there long after basketball was gone.

8.

BORN TO RUN IN THE USA

I arrived at Notre Dame Prep in Fitchburg, Massachusetts, at the end of 2011 to spend one semester playing in the high school league. I expected to be staying at an American version of Scots College given that the name Notre Dame made me think of posh old stone buildings. Instead I found I'd be staying in an absolute shithole.

On the first of the three stories was the kitchen and classrooms, which were actually converted bedrooms because it was originally a house. The teachers lived on the second story and the students lived on the top one. I'm not exaggerating when I say it was straight out of a horror movie.

It's a school that's pretty much for anyone who doesn't score well on the standardized admissions test (SAT) used for college entry in the U.S., which I didn't know at the time. I thought I was going there solely to work on my basketball. It turned out that my SAT results were fine, but I didn't get them back until March and I was sent to Notre Dame in December.

There was a basketball gym, although calling it a gym is a bit generous. It had a green vinyl floor which concealed concrete underneath, so it wasn't exactly great for the joints to be running on that stuff all day. The hoops were old and had half-moon backboards, which I didn't even know still existed.

My teammates were cool, though. We bonded over our crappy shared living experience and the fact this was a new environment for all of us. Our basketball team made up nearly the entire student body. The only students who weren't in the basketball team were three Korean exchange students and one girl who had a baby and had been in juvenile detention.

After being at Scots College, where the academic side is taken very seriously, doing classes aimed at players who had failed most subjects was a piece of cake. Besides, I didn't end up needing extra marks anyway. In fact, it seemed like the school needed us more than we needed it. When we weren't in class or playing basketball, we had to help keep the school running.

The gym was hired out every week for bingo, which we were in charge of setting up. Trestle tables and chairs were brought in and a TV was balanced on one of the rims so everyone could see the numbers when they were called. None of that stuff would ever be allowed on a wooden gym floor, but it's hard to dent concrete by scraping a chair over it.

The place might have put some people off playing basketball at college, but I think most of us there came from fairly rough backgrounds and were used to making do. I might have spent the past four years going to a private school, but that didn't erase my ability to sleep anywhere, no matter how gross.

I did struggle with being alone again, and it was hard not to relapse into the depression I had felt after Dad died. I'd gotten used to having a tight-knit community around me, always willing to help out with anything. At Notre Dame I had nothing but my guitar, which turned into a bit of a lifesaver. For me, the trick to fighting thoughts of loneliness has always been to find a routine. I had a packed routine the whole time I was in Wellington and it had never given me time to sink into self-pity. Once I got to Notre Dame and saw how miserable the whole place was, the door to those repressed emotions became unlocked. If it wasn't for one of the coaches, that door might have swung wide open.

Nick was a coach and a teacher at the school, but pretty soon he became more like a big brother. I think he knew how bad the place was and because I was the biggest and also the only player from outside America, he looked out for me in the form of good food. The meals at the school were truly terrible. Almost every day for lunch we were given gross burger patties on a dry bun. It was like eating Spam, except worse. I would have gladly tucked into a can of Spam. But when you're hungry and have no money to buy other food, you eat what you're given.

Nick must've seen I was struggling because he offered to take me to dinner at his mum's restaurant in town. It was heaven. I ate more that night than I had ever eaten before. After that, Nick took me there for a feed most weekends, and we'd chat about school and life and what I planned to do once I left that hellhole. I've eaten better food at better restaurants since then, but nothing has ever tasted as good as those steaks and pasta did after a week of gray burger patties.

While my life off the court was an ongoing series of disappointments, I made up for it by playing my arse off on the court. We won most of our games, but when you're playing with guys for only a few months there isn't the same team bond that you have with your local high school team or, for me, the Wellington rep team. Instead, everyone was just trying to play well so that they could be included in the discussions around who might be potential draft picks in the next few years.

Playing for Notre Dame was the first time I ever matched up against Nerlens Noel, who, even back then, was being touted as a top-five draft prospect while playing for Tilton, a prep school in New Hampshire. Once again, I went in as a massive underdog and once again I came out of it equal, if not better. A lot of basketball commentators considered that to be my first real test against the top American players and I'm sure they expected me to choke. Just as I believe a lot of New Zealanders were expecting to be disappointed in my performance.

I went into the game knowing that if I was ever going to stamp my name on the collective basketball consciousness, it would be by outplaying Nerlens Noel.

Of course he was good. It took me a few minutes to adjust to his speed, but once I'd sussed out his moves I knew we'd be an even match. We spent the game blocking everyone else on each other's teams but not being able to do much against each other on defense. We basically just showed that we were better than each other's teammates.

Late in the third quarter, Tilton got a steal and they were in transition. I was sprinting back and got to halfway before I saw Nerlens standing under the hoop, waiting for the pass. I knew I couldn't let him get an easy dunk like that so I boosted and got there for the block—my only one on him all game and maybe the one play that edged me in front of him in that contest.

After that game, I knew I had a very real shot at the NBA. If I could match up against a potential number-one draft pick, there was no reason for me not to get drafted too.

When my one semester at Notre Dame was completed, I was allowed to go home for the summer—winter back in New Zealand—before reporting to Pitt in September. I've never been so glad to go home to more cold weather. Being overseas for that long made me miss everyone in Wellington a lot, though not as much as I missed Rotorua and my siblings there. But before I could head to Mohi's farm to live the good life, I had some business to take care of with my Wellington rep team.

They had been messaging me asking if I could play in the under 21 national tournament in May. I wanted to, but I didn't know if I would be back in time or whether under NCAA rules I was even allowed to play. They put my name down on the team roster but expected to play without me for the first time in four years. I got back just in time for the tournament and it was probably just as well. We won the final against North Harbor in overtime.

That night, as we were all drinking out of the trophy and celebrating four consecutive national titles, I got a bit emotional. For three years I had taken for granted that everyone in a basketball team would get along and put the team first. It took leaving New Zealand for me to realize that I probably wouldn't have such a strong bond with my teammates ever again. I'll blame my soppiness on the beers because that was the first time I'd gotten drunk in a while, and I'd only been drunk a handful of times in my life, including the time I got wasted at a cousin's wedding in Rotorua when I was 12.

Playing in that tournament reminded me why I love playing basketball. When you play with your friends it's not work or hard, it's fun. It's obviously more enjoyable when you win every game, so that definitely helped. It was the perfect environment to return to before I showed up at Mohi's farm, where I felt like I was 12 years old all over again.

There was no way of knowing at the time, but that winter at Mohi's farm was the last proper break I would have. I had no responsibilities and nothing at all on my mind except eating, wrestling my brothers, and catching up with my family. It lasted only a couple of weeks, but it was enough to get rid of all the stress that had been building up while I was at Notre Dame. It was hard to worry about the future when my older siblings were treating me like the baby brother I was and taking care of me. After the winter of 2012, that became rarer and rarer.

After my rest and recovery in Rotorua, I was back in Wellington and back in the gym with Kenny. We'd been working on my mid-range shot before I left for Notre Dame and it had served me well over there, so we carried on extending my range. Kenny had seen how big men were becoming perimeter shooters and knew that it was something I'd have to develop eventually, so we decided to start early. A big man who can only dunk isn't hard to guard. I needed an option straight off the pass and a mid-range floater was exactly that. We spent hours shooting from all around the key until it was as comfortable for me as a layup.

The gray burgers and gray mood of Notre Dame meant that as I made my way to Pitt I'd set my expectations low. I was wrong. As soon as I arrived I saw it was awesome. The facilities were better than anything I'd ever experienced, and it felt like a professional organization. Most athletes stay in the freshman dorms, which can get pretty rowdy, but I asked to have my own room. Either everyone was a quiet student where I lived or they had put me with all the nerds. Either way, I liked the quiet.

I'd heard that at colleges known for their sports, the athletic guys get treated like celebrities and go to lots of crazy parties. The dorm I was in didn't have any big parties and the one I did go to when I first arrived was so lame it put me off ever going to another. I'm sure there were cool parties somewhere on campus, but I never saw them. If that's what college party life was like, I was fine being a loser who stayed home every night with my guitar.

I've never been a big drinker, at least not a binge drinker like most of my friends. At Scots there would be parties every weekend and although I had the best intentions of going, when the day of the party came around I'd be too exhausted to go anywhere. One of the only times I got properly drunk, I went to training the next morning and caught a pass with my face. After that I knew drinking wasn't going to do me any favors. I decided to leave it to my friends who weren't trying to make it to the NBA.

Living with the non-athletic students in part got me amped up for the academic side of my scholarship. I'd decided that I still loved farming, so I wanted to study courses that were in that field and maybe even major in agriculture or something similar. But when I went to sign up for classes I found I'd already been put in some of the easiest elective courses. It's a weird situation because I think the athletic department assumed that all the basketball players wanted to do the least schoolwork possible and worked out their timetables for them. I'd seen some science and math courses that I was quite keen to study, but I ended up taking a bunch of social science electives because apparently they are the easiest to pass.

The one thing I learned at Pitt was how good the New Zealand education system is. I'd developed good study and learning habits at Scots and when I got to Pitt I found I didn't even need them. Most of the assignments I had to do were opinionated answers or self-reflection for which you didn't need to do any research. I basically didn't go to school. I'd just go to the exam, write an essay on what I thought about a topic, and get really good grades.

I eventually got drawn into studying music because that was at least an interest of mine, but I found it difficult. I can play any song on the guitar by just listening to it a few times, but studying music meant learning how to read and write the notes. That was like learning a new language and I struggled. It was the same as me struggling to write down my ideas. I know how to do it, I just find it hard to get things down on paper.

By the end of my second semester at Pitt I was awarded a prize for academic achievement by a student athlete. It's a nice-looking award and it sits on a shelf at home where everyone who visits is impressed by it. But I feel I can't really claim it because I know I barely did any schoolwork. If I was able to get an award for academic achievement after doing hardly any work, I hate to think what sort of learning every other student athlete was doing. Ironically, that award serves as a daily reminder of why getting an education should be at the top of every young athlete's priorities.

What little work all the basketball players were doing in the classroom was made up for by the workload in the gym. I knew that college conditioning would be a step up from my Wellington training, but the preseason training period at Pitt was the hardest I've ever worked out in my life. I called it "meathead training" because it felt like they were trying to make us all huge in the gym, and I didn't see the point of it. I liked the competition, though. Put a bunch of athletes in a weight room and they'll turn into beasts trying to outlift each other.

Once we had finished in the weight room, we would do our conditioning tests. It always started out simple enough, a few sprints and slides to warm up. Then the torture started with 21 suicides.

Everyone who has ever played basketball in a proper team knows what a suicide is. I'm sure someone has come up with a more PC name for it now, but it will always be a suicide to me. It's a simple but effective sprint workout that's usually brought out as a punishment if a team is training badly or has played poorly in a game. Players line up on the baseline and when the whistle blows everyone sprints to the free-throw line, touches the ground with a hand, then sprints back to the baseline. Then they do the same to the halfway line and back to the baseline, to the far free-throw line and back to the baseline, to the far baseline and back. That counts as one suicide. It's monotonous and the worst.

This conditioning test comprised one suicide every minute for 21 minutes. The faster we ran them, the more rest we got before the minute was up. Bigs are never expected to do as well as guards in these drills, but the competitive beast in me made sure that I was always either leading or near the front in every drill, including the 21 suicides.

Straight after that we did sixers, which involves sprinting six lengths of the court, then sprinting backwards for two lengths and then sprinting six lengths again. You had to do that under a certain time limit after the 21 suicides, which not everyone made. I was one of the faster bigs, but some of them didn't get there. It absolutely destroyed us. If you consider yourself to be pretty fit, go run 21 suicides in 21 minutes. It'll make you question every decision you ever made. It definitely made me wonder why I ever wanted to be a professional basketball player.

In those first few months at Pitt I thought seriously about chucking it all in, quitting America and going home to New Zealand where I was more comfortable. Anything to avoid agony every day from conditioning. I knew that I was ahead of the pack, at least for the bigs, but that didn't make it any less of a nightmare. I felt I wasn't at the level I was supposed to be at, which bugged me, but at the same time I could see that if I wasn't then no one else was either.

I would say that at least half of what I was feeling was in fact homesickness and nothing to do with the basketball. More and more Kiwi kids are getting scholarships to good colleges in America, but some of them return to New Zealand within the first 100 days, which I totally understand. It's not easy being completely alone in a new school as well as a new country. The usual advice to make friends and create a family didn't work for me. I got through it with sheer determination and the knowledge that it wasn't forever. If it would get me to a career in basketball, I was willing to put up with some lonely, painful years.

In October, before the season officially began, Pitt held a Midnight Madness event. It is basically a huge rally to kick off the season with a bit of dumb stuff thrown in. New Zealanders don't support amateur sports the way Americans do so I had never seen anything like the thousands of people who showed up to watch a bunch of teenagers perform some silly skits. Coach Dixon dressed up as Will Ferrell's character Jackie Moon in *Semi-Pro* and roasted us. The team held a dunk contest, which I didn't enter because my dunks back then were quite lame. The closest I got to the glory was being jumped over by the winner during an encore dunk.

Pitt was one of the top colleges in the country, but even then we were predicted to come in only sixth in our Big East Conference. Things started well for us—almost too well. We won our first four games convincingly, though none were Big East rivals. By the time we played our first major rival in Cincinnati on New Year's Eve, we had gotten used to winning comfortably. So of course we lost, 70–61. Against Rutgers University from New Jersey a few days later, we lost again. This time we had 26 three-point attempts and only made eight of them. Coach Dixon was playing a small game, but in that match-up, the small game failed miserably.

Soon I was already not enjoying basketball and it only got worse from there. After years of working on expanding my shooting game, I was told not to shoot. To Coach Dixon, I was a big man for rebounds and dunks and nothing else. Kenny had spent countless hours drilling into me that no matter what position you play, you should have a full skillset. But pretty quickly I found my skillset diminishing as the bigs only worked on "big" stuff and had no time for shooting or ball handling. If I shot a mid-range floater—my new favorite shot—during a game, I'd be told off and benched. If you watch my short highlights video from my time playing for Pitt, every single basket is either a dunk or a putback right by the rim. That wasn't the game I wanted to play; it was the game I was forced to play. It's no wonder I led the team in field goal percentage.

I also frequently led games in rebounds because what else was I going to do? In three games I got 14 rebounds and in one I pulled in 15. After one of those games, Coach Dixon spoke again about how I needed to improve further. I agreed with him on that at least, but I knew he wanted me to improve on my own somehow when I've always needed a mentor to push me. That's what playing for the Saints did back in Wellington.

For our last game in January 2013 we traveled to Kentucky to play the University of Louisville, the number-one ranked team in the Big East Conference. We knew they would be a force, but we also knew we had all the tools to beat them. More than 22,000 local fans turned out, which is more than you'll find at most NBA playoff games. I couldn't believe that many people wanted to see a bunch of teenagers play basketball. It was a close game, which we lost right at the end, 64–61.

I had a quiet game, but what made that game special was playing against Peyton Siva. I didn't mark him, as he was a point guard, and I barely spoke to him, but I had seen his last name and recognized it as being Samoan. In the U.S., it's not often two young Pacific Islanders play basketball against each other in front of 22,000 people and have it aired on national television.

We finished off the regular season with good wins over Syracuse University and University of Cincinnati, who were both ranked above us, before traveling to Madison Square Garden, New York City, to play our first round of the Big East Tournament, the championship tournament of the Big East Conference, against Syracuse (again). We couldn't deliver on the day and lost 62–59. We were out.

For the NCAA Division I tournament, or March Madness as it's more commonly known, we were seeded eighth. With 64 teams involved and every round being a knockout, I can see why March Madness draws such massive viewing numbers every year. At eighth seed in our regional bracket of 16 teams—there are four brackets and the winner of each proceeds to the final four—we were pegged to be one of the closer games. The first seed has the advantage of playing the sixteenth seed first up, the second seed plays the fifteenth seed, and so on. We were scheduled to play Wichita State University, who were ninth seed, in our first match. Technically, we were the favorites, but they weren't in our conference so we had no idea how tough they would be. What we did know is that there are upsets every year at March Madness so no game can be taken for granted.

All season, one of just two seniors in our team, Tray Woodall, had been our standout player. He often led the scoring and was always the playmaker for us. Against Wichita State he shot one from 12 and ended up with two points. We lost 73–55. I don't know what happened for Tray that night, but I felt for the guy. It ended up being his last game playing for Pitt and, as he said himself, the worst game he'd ever played.

I suddenly found myself with more ball than I'd had the whole season. I did what I'd been doing all season and ended up being the leading point scorer for our team with 13 points and 11 rebounds. I wasn't all that surprised that I was able to step up. I find that when I'm forced to play above what I'm used to, I can adapt to the situation and not make a fool of myself. The thing was, up until that night, I'd never been given enough responsibility to force me to level up. In fact, the opposite had happened.

In reality, my freshman college season was pretty good. I put up decent numbers and didn't show any major weaknesses. But because I hadn't enjoyed it, I finished our final game just relieved to be getting a break.

I had complained to Kenny a lot during that season, and he promised he would start looking for other college options after I told him there was no way I could play for four years being so restricted. Since then I've heard that some top coaches will restrict a potential draft pick in their freshman year because it forces them to return to the school the following year. So much NBA scouting is done at college games that if a top freshman looks like they are underperforming, they are less likely to declare early for the draft. I hope it wasn't true in my case, but I definitely felt I hadn't reached my full potential that first season.

During our final media session of the season, yet another reporter asked me if I would be returning for my sophomore year at Pitt. I told them that of course I was coming back. "I don't know why you guys keep asking that question, man," I said. "I'm coming back."

Twelve days later I declared for the 2013 NBA draft.

9.

READY FOR THE BIG LEAGUES

The moment I stop enjoying basketball, I'll quit. Things were heading that way when I was at Pitt, and if there was one thing I knew it was that I had to leave before it ruined the game for me forever. Talking to Kenny since, I've learned that he always planned for me to be at Pitt for just one year.

The draft of 2013 has been ranked as one of the weakest in NBA history, or at least in recent history. The 2012 draft had Anthony Davis, Bradley Beal, Damian Lillard, Andre Drummond, and Draymond Green, who have all played in at least one NBA All-Star game. The 2011 draft had Kyrie Irving, Kemba Walker, Klay Thompson, Kawhi Leonard, Jimmy Butler, and Isaiah Thomas. The only All-Stars from the 2013 draft so far are Victor Oladipo and Giannis Antetokounmpo, who was drafted at 15 by the Milwaukee Bucks. It's funny to think of that guy being drafted at 15 because he's an absolute beast now and I'm sure he will be an MVP at some point.

You just can never tell with something as subjective as a draft, but Kenny had done his research and studied the classes for each year and he had determined that my best shot at being drafted was in 2013. If I had loved playing at Pitt and felt it was good for my game, I might have stayed. Instead, I announced my intention to declare for the draft and got myself an agent, meaning there was no going back. Once you have an agent, you are no longer an amateur and therefore can't play for a college team. I signed the contract with the Wasserman agency without hesitating for a second.

I told Kenny that no matter what we decided to do, I needed to get back to New Zealand. Preparing for the draft was going to be a full-time job and I couldn't go straight into that after a less than satisfactory year of basketball. Kenny spoke to my new agent, Mats, and told him that I'd be doing some of my draft training in New Zealand. Surprise, surprise—Mats didn't think that was a good idea. America is the best in the world at basketball so having some Kiwi kid say he is going to prepare for the NBA in Wellington wouldn't exactly fill anyone with confidence. Kenny managed to convince him that if I began my preparations in New Zealand, I would be re-energized and more enthusiastic when I came back for the draft combine testing.

And so on the day the basketball world found out that I had declared for the draft, I was hunting pigs in Rotorua. That week spent back home with my family saved me. I still wasn't used to people seeing me as something of a celebrity, so it made all the difference to be around people who couldn't care less and who just wanted to spend time with me. A bunch of us went to visit Dad's grave. I'd been using basketball and school to push back my grief for five years, but standing there, about to start a massive new journey in my life, it hit me again just how much I missed the old man.

After five days of doing nothing but eating and sleeping—the first time I'd had consecutive days off in a while—I flew to Wellington to start my preparations for the draft. As soon as I landed, Kenny took me straight to see Gavin Cross, my trainer.

I first met Gavin (Gav to his friends) in 2009 when I was 16. I was already a year into my training and had a personal trainer in Blossom, but Kenny wanted me to see Gav for any physio needs I might have. At that point I'd never been injured, but with me at 6'9" and still growing, Kenny was worried about how my joints were handling all the activity.

I liked Gav from our first meeting. He's small and Welsh, and he knows everything there is to know about the body and how it functions. Right from the beginning he would explain everything to me. If I know the why then I'm fully engaged. Kenny had told Gav to keep me involved in my own wellbeing, and he did that by explaining every single thing to me. If we did a new workout, he showed me the exact muscles we were working and why they were important for me to strengthen. He followed through by doing the workouts with me and that's what sealed the deal. Not only did I know that Gav knew what he was talking about, I saw that he was willing to put in literally the same amount of work to get me to my fittest self.

When I arrived in Wellington I was booked to fly to Los Angeles two weeks later. The first thing Gav did when he saw me was shake his head. I'd gotten bigger during my year at Pitt, but it was all up top. Most colleges work their athletes in the gym just to get big. I had been talking to Gav occasionally from the U.S. and he wasn't a fan of the workouts they were having me do. But I knew better than to undermine a coach, so I told him I would be doing whatever the Pitt team asked of me and then when I saw him again we would pick up where we had left off. Well, that all changed when I returned from Pitt looking like an upside-down pyramid. The extra strength was good, but it was in all the wrong places.

Gav had been prepped by Kenny so when I arrived in Wellington we got straight into it. We were working to a 10-week program. It was 10 weeks until the bulk of my workouts with NBA teams so I wanted to be at my fittest by mid-June. However, the draft combine testing—which would be the first chance to show my fitness and strength—was mid-May, so the first stage of the journey was to get me ready for that. Gav looked me up and down and said I needed to trim some weight from up top and work on strengthening my core. And then there was the bench press.

The combine testing is supposed to reveal athletes' physical strengths and weaknesses. Most of the tests make sense, like sprints, agility runs, and vertical leaps. But they also do a bench press test, which doesn't have much to do with basketball. The test is to see how many reps you can do at 185 lbs (84 kg). In 2007, Kevin Durant couldn't even do one rep and look at him now. I was no Kevin Durant so I trained for that stupid test, even though I had pretty much never used a bench press in training.

We wasted no time getting me to train like I was already in the NBA. Each day began at 6 a.m. shooting with Kenny, much like when I was at school. He immediately reintroduced mid-range shooting and I shot endless sets from 15 feet (5 meters) every day. That was also a testing distance for the combine. After my morning shootaround, I would have a big breakfast and then work out with Gav for an hour at 11 a.m.

It was in this pre-draft training period that Gav introduced me to Tabata workouts, which are a form of high-intensity interval training. They are designed to be short but hell, with 20 seconds of intense effort then 10 seconds' rest, repeated at least eight times. The exercises usually rely on bodyweight, but Gav had me do them with weights to build my overall strength. He even had me work out barefoot to improve my balance and foot strength. Every last area was covered.

Those workouts were probably just as painful as the conditioning at Pitt and yet I actually enjoyed them because my brother Sid would come and work out with me. It became sort of fun to almost die during a quick Tabata workout and then look at each other knowing we'd smashed it. It didn't take long for my weight to move around and drop off. After working out with Gav, I'd go home for another feed and maybe a nap, then head back into town for yoga or a spin class with Blossom. Then it was back to the gym for another shootaround with Kenny to finish the day. It was full on, but I knew exactly what it was for, so I just knuckled down and got to work. I wasn't going to let complacency lead to me being undrafted come June.

In just two weeks, I felt like my fitness, energy, and enthusiasm for the game were at an all-time high. That's a testament to Kenny and Gav's coaching skills. They were able to attack the challenge together in a way they knew was best for me. It was like I had reset and reconnected with why I started playing in the first place. When Kenny and I flew to Los Angeles to set up a base for the pre-draft workouts, I felt at the top of my game.

My agency put Kenny and me up in an apartment down the road from UCLA, where I worked out before the combine and in between team workouts. I worked out in LA with other players who were represented by Wasserman, and at one of the trainings one of the top agents came to watch. At the end of the workout he came over and started squeezing my cheeks like a baby, saying "I love you" over and over. Then he went to Kenny and did the same thing. I guess he saw some big dollar signs hanging over me or something, but if he was happy, I was happy.

For the next month I worked out every day with Kenny and the Wasserman crew, and did Gav's Tabata workouts whenever I could, in my room or off to the side of the court. He had designed them specifically so they didn't need any equipment and I could do them virtually anywhere. It wasn't as much fun doing them by myself, but they were short enough that I could power through them and be on to something different before I started feeling sorry for myself. Meanwhile, I kept working on my mid-range shots day in and day out.

At the end of April 2013, Kenny got us tickets to a Lakers game. He grew up playing with Magic Johnson's brother so I got to experience my first ever NBA game from Magic's suite. I loved it, but more for the amazing food and comfortable seats than the actual game, which I barely watched. I've never watched a lot of basketball and probably never will. I always have enough basketball on my own plate that I don't need to watch more of it in my spare time, no matter how good the players are. But it was a fun night out being in the fancy corporate box.

The combine testing was held in Chicago over five days in the middle of May and was my first chance to work out in front of NBA scouts and executives. For players who have an incredible college career under their belt, the combine is simply a place to remind coaches and scouts that you've got skills. But for relatively unknown players like me, the combine can be the launching pad for a career if you impress enough people and get your name in the mix of top prospects. I didn't think that anyone was going to draft me based solely on my one underwhelming college season, so I had to blow everyone away at the combine.

Meeting my draft classmates was fascinating. Nobody really socialized, yet we all had so much in common we should have been mates. I minded my own business and concentrated on acing the first tests, which were the sprints and the bench press. I managed 16 reps in the bench test, which was the third best in the group. It's completely pointless and I'm sure a lot of players didn't even bother training for it for that very reason, but coming third in that test put my name near the top of a list somewhere, so it was worth the focus in training just for the exposure.

In the vertical leap and short sprints, I scored near the lower end, but I expected that because guards are meant to be faster, more agile, and more explosive than bigs. I was happy with my performances, though, as they were always at the top of the bigs leaderboard. Cody Zeller, who is also a center, was like some sort of alien and managed to lead in pretty much every test, even against the guards. There wasn't much anyone else could do but marvel at his athleticism and dream of having a 35.5-inch (90-cm) standing vertical leap.

I wasn't fazed, though, because I knew the shooting drills would be my time to shine. And I was right. In the stationary 15-foot shooting test and the roaming shooting I felt like I couldn't miss. There were a couple of guys who had absolute mares in the shooting drills and I felt stink for them, but I was on fire.

The rest of the week was spent getting medical tests done. Apparently, I have long lungs. And you know what they say about guys with long lungs...nothing. They say nothing. As well as being poked and prodded and scanned like guinea pigs, we met with a bunch of different teams. I remember the Dallas Mavericks meeting vividly because they had a psychologist present who asked some pretty strange questions. It was fun, though, and different from the other team meetings. By the end of the week, I felt like I knew what teams were looking for and how to promote my strengths effectively.

I also felt like I nailed the media portion of the combine. It's not listed as a test and there's no grading, but any team that is remotely interested in a player will watch their combine interview. For a lot of players, particularly the ones who weren't college superstars, it's the first time they experience a media scrum, which is a huge part of NBA life. If you come off as a dick in your interview, scouts will note it down. It wasn't something I particularly "trained" for, but I had definitely been thinking about it and talking to Kenny about how I should approach it. If you go back and watch my interview on YouTube, I look like a five-year-old being asked if he likes going to Disneyland. All my answers are innocent and unassuming. Now I'm not saying I was acting, but I'm no idiot.

I knew that the media loved the fact that I was relatively new to the game and didn't talk myself up the way some other players did. So just like you would be your best self in a job interview, I put on my best self for that combine interview. And at that time, my best self was my most naive, humble, I'm-just-here-to-have-fun self. It was all true, but I definitely played it up a little. Wouldn't you?

It must have worked because the Bleacher Report website did a write-up that same day to determine the winners and losers of the 2013 combine and named me as the biggest winner, specifically mentioning my shooting and my interview. Just a few days earlier I was at best a long-term project who might go somewhere in the middle of the first round. Now people were looking at me differently. Maybe, just maybe, I could be drafted in the top 10.

Now all I had to do was impress the coaches at team workouts for the next month. Easier said than done.

10.

PRE-DRAFT WORKOUT DIARY

Monday, 20 May 2013

Back in LA, training with all the draft players represented by the Wasserman agency. There's quite a few of us. Had a chill day after a full-on week at the combine. It's as hot as in California, but luckily our place has a pool so fellow draft hopeful Ray McCallum and I had a swim between workouts. I've been getting sent so much gear from sponsors there's no more room in my closet. Have just started a pile of adidas T-shirts and shoes on the floor of my room. There's at least 20 pairs there and I'll probably wear two of them. I'm not really a shoe guy, but it's nice to have options rather than searching everywhere for a pair that fits. It took six years for me to go from having everything I owned fit in a sports bag to having so many sports bags and shoes that it's actually a bit annoying. First-world problems, eh?

Friday, 24 May 2013

The agency was given tickets to the premiere of *Now You See Me*, a blockbuster film about magicians. I went along with the boys and we got to see some of the stars of the movie, including Isla Fisher. Mate, actors are way smaller in real life than they look in movies. I wore the outfit we'd picked out for my team interviews. It's the only nice outfit I own. A lavender shirt was a bold choice, but I have a feeling I'm gonna get sick of it real soon. My sweat marks show up hard out on it.

Saturday, 25 May 2013

In Boston for my first NBA team workout. I thought Pitt had the flashest facilities but the Celtics' place was mean as. Kevin Garnett and Paul Pierce had massage chairs at their lockers. I guess that's what you get when you're a legend.

The workout was straightforward enough, pretty much a regular morning training with shooting drills and then short scrimmages. At the end of the 90-minute workout we had to do the three-minute run test, otherwise referred to by players as the Boston Marathon. It's very simple—they put three minutes on the clock and you just run from baseline to baseline as many times as you can. It's basic but it's very, very tough. I don't remember how many I got, I just know I didn't come in last so was happy with that. They're not necessarily worried about how many lengths you manage; I think they use it to see how players push themselves at the very end of a workout or game. You'll never catch me in cruise mode so I knew even if I did come in last they'd see me giving 100 percent right to the end, which probably counted for more. Credit where credit's due, Mike Muscala got the most lengths.

Thursday, 30 May 2013

Worked out for the Dallas Mavericks today. I thought the Celtics had flash facilities but, mate, it's a whole different ball game in the middle of the country. Did a video tour of the place and posted it on my Facebook page for my friends and family back home to see. I've basically been given a trip to outer space—of course I'm gonna try filming it so my mates can experience it too. It's also good for me because otherwise there's no one else to buzz out with about the NBA teams. The other draft guys are never as impressed by the mini Red Bull fridges as I am.

The workout was almost the same as in Boston except better, because I got to talk to old mate Dirk Nowitzki afterwards. I don't watch much NBA, but I've seen enough of Dirk to know he's the man. He was the first seven-footer I saw who could knock down threes as well. I have a mid-range shot but, mate, imagine if I developed a three-point game.

Saturday, 1 June 2013

I came back to LA for the Wasserman draft workout, which was a special run put on by my agency to showcase about six of us to all their clients. It was almost like a second combine but more relaxed and just like a regular training with spectators. Luckily, I didn't wear my contacts so I couldn't recognize any of the faces from the different teams. They may as well have been randos off the street for all I knew.

Sunday, 2 June 2013

Excited to be in Oklahoma City for a couple of days. Things are picking up and I'm now taking flights pretty much every day. It's not like New Zealand where flights are 45 minutes; these are the real deal. As soon as I arrived I went through a medical to make sure I'm healthy. Thank God I've got no hidden injuries. The place reminds me of New Zealand, just not on the coast. In fact, it's basically smack bang in the middle of America. It's good to see some real green grass again, though.

Monday, 3 June 2013

Just finished my workout for the Thunder and tried to take a video of their mean-as facilities but got told by Russell Westbrook that I wasn't allowed. He might've been lying, but I wasn't about to argue with him. That's how you know an organization is hard out, when they won't even let people take photos inside or with their players. I really liked their vibe, though. The bigs coach, Mark Bryant, talked me through the tape of our workout and pointed out things I could improve on. Will be working on those from now on.

They were so hospitable, kinda like Pacific people. Every little thing was taken care of, and I felt like I was visiting an aunt who wouldn't stop fussing over me. It's the closest thing to a Kiwi vibe I've felt so far so would be awesome to be drafted there. Doesn't hurt that they made the NBA finals two years ago either.

Tuesday, 4 June 2013

Flew east and am now in Philadelphia with the 76ers. Usually there'll be a group of five or six players working out together for each organization, but I seem to be the only one here, which is weird. My aunty from Wellington sent me a pounamu necklace that I now wear everywhere to represent New Zealand.

I gotta say, the Philadelphia visit has been weird. It was as professional as all the other organizations, but even I could tell there's something happening with the staff here. The head coach and general manager both left at the end of last season, so the new coach and GM are still getting on the same page as everyone else. On top of that, they share their facilities with a medical school so there were random medical students in the weight room and playing ping-pong while we worked out. Don't get me wrong, that's totally chill and I'm not high maintenance like that. But I know I would benefit the most being in a team that's already established and stable.

Friday, 7 June 2013

Worked out with the Utah Jazz today in the Mormon capital of America, and maybe the world. I know there are a lot of Pacific Islanders who live in Utah because many of them are Mormon, so I'm sure I'll see some distant Tongan relatives soon enough. Starting to get a collection of T-shirts from each team and just realized I won't be allowed to wear any of them once I'm signed to an organization. Seems like a waste of good clothes.

Monday, 10 June 2013

Okay, I lied. The Cleveland Cavaliers have the best facilities in the NBA. Sadly, they were also too flash to let me record, which I'm starting to think is the sign of a good, tight-knit organization. Most of the gear was pretty much the same as in Texas and Oklahoma, except the whole place looked like a giant log cabin. For a bush-man like me, that rich mahogany will win me over every time.

Tuesday, 11 June 2013

Working out with the Timberwolves in Minnesota. They had food and water waiting on my bed at the hotel when I arrived so they get bonus points for that. I was excited because I'd seen Cody Zeller on the list of players working out that day. I hadn't worked out with anyone who was a predicted top-10 pick, let alone a top-10 center, so I was keen to go up against him. He'd wasted me and everyone else in basically every physical test at the combine and I wanted redemption.

Yesterday I saw him and asked if he was working out and he said, "Yeah," so I prepared myself. Mate, I'm super competitive and this guy had outperformed me at everything a month ear-lier. Of course I was psyching myself up. Then we start working out this morning and I look over and he's just standing on the sideline, watching. I was pissed off, man. Maybe his team heard that I was known to be physical during workouts and didn't want him to get injured. A lot of people have been talking about how I'm doing really well in workouts. The worst thing for Cody, a top-five prospect, would be for me, a shaky top-15 prospect, to beat him in a scrimmage. They probably didn't want to risk his stock dropping. I dunno, whatever his reasons, I didn't care. I was just annoyed that I had no other center to work out with.

Thursday, 13 June 2013

Chicago had the most inspiring facilities just because of Michael Jordan and knowing that was his home. The Bulls' practice gym was filled with massive banners of all their past champion-ships and inspirational moments. I'm a sucker for inspirational banners.

Friday, 14 June 2013

I'm so sweaty. Trying to cool down in Phoenix, Arizona, where it's 40 degrees Celsius. Mate, that's just too hot. Don't know how anyone plays an outdoor sport here—it's an actual desert. The Suns are cool and a lot like the Celtics (there's some crossover with the staff). They even did the three-minute run test at the end of our workout too. Again, don't know what I got this time, and don't really care, but I was out of it by the end. I like their coach, though; he seems really onto it.

Feel like Phoenix is definitely a possibility with the fifth pick. They're looking for a big guy and they liked my workout so maybe they could go for me. But have just heard I'm heading back to OKC tonight for a second visit. It's all supposed to be top secret so they're flying me to a random place and *then* to Okla-homa City, so that the Phoenix guys don't see where I'm going. Might as well just call me Mr. Bond from now on.

Saturday, 15 June 2013

Back in OKC for a second secret workout and this time it's liter-ally just me. I trained with Mark Bryant again and tried to show him that I'd been working on the things he told me during my first Thunder workout. I think he was quite impressed that I'd remembered. They then made me sit down with a psychologist and answer a bunch of weird questions that I don't really think had anything to do with basketball. How many golf balls would fit inside a bus? Uhhhhhhh. Maybe they wanted to make sure I wasn't a psychopath or something. They could've just asked.

The first workout had been a test of my physical abilities and work on the court, but the second workout felt like they were testing me out as a person to see if I'd fit with the group. If that's what all teams do, I guess my only hope is the Thunder. Something tells me they're unique like that, wanting to triple-check every decision. That fits with their vibe.

Someone on Facebook asked me which team I wanted to be drafted to and I replied the San Antonio Spurs. At least half of all basketball players in New Zealand would be Spurs fans. Mohi's a massive Spurs fan so I take his word that they're the best. Why? Because their style of play is the closest in the NBA to New Zealand's style. We never have teenagers who can do all these fancy moves and then posterize someone. We just run a motion and look for the open cutter or open shot. So to see someone like their coach Gregg Popovich, who is just so cool, leading the Spurs to championships was amazing to watch in New Zealand.

The Spurs haven't asked me to work out for them, which cuts me real deep. I just want a chance to give Pop a hug, that's all.

Tuesday, 18 to Sunday, 23 June 2013

I worked out with the Atlanta Hawks, Portland Trail Blazers, and Sacramento Kings in the final week before the draft. They were all great organizations, but the workouts felt a bit like afterthoughts, as if they figured they may as well see me train just in case. All three of them are supposedly not even looking for a center, at least not with their first picks. But it was good to get in more gym time, and I got to spend more time folding my legs into airplane seats.

I've done so many workouts it's ridiculous. I think my situation is unique in that my ranking at the beginning of the draft process is very different from my ranking now. Before the combine there were some interested teams, but I definitely wasn't considered to be a high draft pick. Then I surprised everyone at the combine and suddenly a lot more teams with high picks were interested in having me work out for them.

Most of the guys who are the "stars" and predicted to go somewhere in the top 10 only work out for a few teams, usually the ones with the highest picks, who are looking to fill their position. If you're ranked that high already, you almost don't want people to see you play more because the only way to go is down. After the combine I was ranked near the top 10, but it was all new so I just said yes to every single workout, partly because I didn't trust the ranking system and partly because I wanted to see as many of the teams as possible. To me, only working out for a couple of teams and turning down the rest would've been like going to Disneyland and going on just two rides. I'm way too cheap to waste a free trip like that.

A lot of organizations would ask which players had impressed me of those I'd worked out with. I always said either Mike Muscala or Rudy Gobert, mainly because I worked out with them the most and they seemed to work as hard as I did. I shouted Rudy lunch at Atlanta airport (I think it was Atlanta) and we had a nice chat about the whole experience. I also had lunch with Dewayne Dedmon after a team workout and he was cool as. It's hard to develop proper friendships with guys you only see on the court while you're competing, but I can't imagine not liking any of those guys from my draft class. They're all good dudes.

Tuesday, 25 June 2013

On the red-eye from LA to New York. By the time we land the draft will be tomorrow night. This past month has been the most fun I've ever had playing basketball, and nothing can take away from that. I get to see Sid and Mohi in New York too, which will be mean.

No matter what happens tomorrow, it'll be fine. Even if nobody, not a single team, wants me, it'll be fine. I'll still have the amazing experience of getting to visit and work out for 11 of the best basketball teams in the world. I'll still have the knowledge that I can go up against NBA players and hold my own. I'll still have the tools and moves that some of the NBA's best coaches have shown me over the past couple of months. And I'll still have all the free gear.

I'll head back to New Zealand, have a break, maybe do a bit of study, then go to Europe to play in the league over there. Eventually, I'll return to America and try to crack the NBA again. I've got patience; they won't be getting rid of me that easily.

But I'm confident that I showed those teams everything I had to offer and that one of them will take a gamble on me. My life up until now has relied on people investing in me, whether with money or time or both, with the faith that I will continue to get better. It has worked so far and with the right team it will keep working. But I'll find all that out tomorrow. For now, I think I've earned a nap.

11.

A NEW HOME IN MIDDLE AMERICA

I forgot how much I missed my hori brothers until I saw them looking very out of place in the middle of Manhattan. It was the first time I had seen my siblings outside New Zealand and it felt like we were on some sort of adventure.

I was predicted to go in the top 15 of the draft, so I was assigned to the green room floor and given a table to fill. Of course, I had to have Kenny and my agent Mats there, but the NBA was willing to pay for three family members to travel to Brooklyn for the big night. I knew straight away that I wanted Sid, Mohi, and Viv there with me.

I wanted to make it a surprise for Mohi so I messaged him saying that I wasn't going to the NBA anymore and to forget about the draft. Since I was 15 years old, Mohi had been asking if he could come to the draft with me when I went. There was no *if* I went, it was always "when you go to the draft." He was the biggest NBA fan and the biggest Steven Adams fan, so of course he had to come. However, my surprise backfired quickly when I looked at my phone an hour later and saw a bunch of missed calls and messages from him asking what was going on. When I told him it was just a joke and he was coming to the draft, all expenses paid, he was still a bit annoyed. "You had me freaking out, you punk."

I didn't even bother trying to surprise Sid, I just told him straight up and he was as chill as always. The big phone call was to Viv, who had been my mum when my actual mum wasn't there. She was always the proudest of me and Val, as if we were her own children, and I knew she'd lose her mind if she got to come to the draft. I told her to keep it a secret because no one was supposed to know, so naturally she told the whole extended family and probably the checkout workers at the supermarket too.

I had my three people and I was ready to show them all the hype that I'd been experiencing on my own. But then Viv called to say that she couldn't come anymore because she couldn't get a U.S. travel visa at such short notice. She was devastated. I asked Mats if he could do anything, but it was too late. The draft was in a few days and flights had to be booked that day.

I tried not to dwell on our missing mate and instead did my best to show Sid and Mohi a good time in New York City. I took them to a restaurant that I had been to before that had a 48-ounce (1.4-kg) steak challenge. I'd already clocked it and had my photo on the wall as proof, but I wanted to see Mohi try because I wasn't sure he could. He nailed it easy and was even wearing an OKC Thunder T-shirt. When I posted a photo of him at dinner on my Facebook page there were a lot of comments speculating whether the T-shirt meant I already knew where I was going. The answer is no.

Mohi had drawn up his own mock draft and predicted that I would be picked by OKC. Then when we were shopping earlier that day he found some NBA T-shirts in a bargain bin, so he bought a Thunder one and wore it to dinner because all his regular clothes smelt like cow shit. It was a complete coincidence but pretty cool when I look back on it now.

I made sure to always wear my T-shirt from the combine testing just to be safe, even though it was getting quite gross. After dinner we went bowling and hung out, enjoying having no responsibilities. It was one of the best nights I had all year.

On draft day it felt like the whole of New York was talking about it. It was like when the All Blacks were in the Rugby World Cup final in New Zealand and you couldn't go anywhere without hearing people discuss the game. Because I'm so tall, a lot of random people guessed that I was in town for the draft and wished me luck.

As we were putting on our suits for the ceremony, I suddenly missed Viv again. She would have been fussing over us and telling us to scrub our toes again. Instead it was just us boys in the hotel room trying to figure out how to tie our ties.

At Barclays Center we walked onto the green room floor, the first New Zealanders to ever do so, and sat down to wait for a feed that never came. People kept thinking Mohi was my dad, which was correct in a sense but also a massive burn on him since he's not that much older than me. As players started getting drafted, we just sat there and fidgeted. Mohi was in heaven and soaking up the atmosphere. Sid and I were too nervous and hungry to do anything but wait impatiently for the next pick.

It took an hour to get to the twelfth pick—the second-longest hour of my life after the hour of suicide tests at Pitt—then five minutes for Oklahoma City to decide and a split second for me to go from being unemployed to being a millionaire NBA player.

Adrenaline carried me through the next three hours and then stripped me of my memory; I now can't recall anything I said to the dozens of reporters I spoke to that night. When we eventually got back to our hotel rooms, Mohi, Sid, and I just sat there grinning at each other. We didn't know what to say because we were living a reality that was so far from what we grew up in we almost couldn't comprehend it. I know Mohi was buzzing out that I'd be on the same team as Kevin Durant and Russell Westbrook. I was buzzing out that I was actually going to be in the NBA at all.

That night I saw Andre Roberson, who had also been drafted by OKC in the first round. We hadn't seen each other in workouts because he was a small forward and I was a big, but he seemed chill. "It's just Dre," he said when he introduced himself. I didn't have a cool nickname so I said nothing. The next day on the plane, his family met mine and I knew if the two of us could stick around we'd be good mates in no time.

Oklahoma City had been the closest I got to feeling like I was back at home during the draft workouts so I felt happy to be heading back there. We showed up with just our suitcases and the Thunder took care of everything else. They organized a realtor to take Kenny and me house hunting, although we couldn't think about buying yet. Oklahoma is so affordable that we could easily afford to rent homes in a nice gated community. The realtor asked me if I was looking for anything in particular. I nearly laughed out loud. The fact that someone was asking me what I preferred in a home was hilarious. I'd barely had my own room and now I'd have a whole house. I told her some high doorways would be nice, and a big backyard.

One of the early downsides to living in Oklahoma City that I noticed was the lack of washing lines. Every place we looked at had big backyards but no clothesline for hanging washing. When I asked the agent about it, she said it's because the winters would freeze the clothes and, besides, no one has time to hang out washing when they can just put it in a clothes dryer. I couldn't help thinking: that's next-level laziness. I didn't trust dryers anyway after one shrunk my training clothes in Dallas and I had to meet Dirk Nowitzki in what felt like a crop top. Luckily, the team at the training facilities said they would wash all our training gear every day for us.

We found a nice place the first day and I left Kenny in charge of sorting furniture. He headed down to a massive homeware store and went crazy. The Thunder had given me an allowance for that stuff—otherwise I probably still wouldn't have any furniture to this day. The one thing I did make sure to get was a custom-made bed. Up to that point in my life I had never slept on a bed that was long enough for me, and if I was going to spend my money on anything, it was going to be that. When it arrived a few weeks later, it was massive. I slept like a baby.

Dre and I were only in the city for a few days before we flew out to Orlando for NBA Summer League. But those few days were enough for me to decide that Oklahoma City was the perfect place for me. And it was the perfect place because it was boring.

That sounds like an unkind thing to say, but I mean it as a compliment. To be fair, it's not so much boring as it is relatively free of distractions. I was a young kid at the start of his career who suddenly didn't have to worry about money. The worst thing for me would have been to move to a city with a thousand events on every night and a lot of places to spend all that money. I didn't have expensive tastes, but that doesn't mean I wouldn't have gotten distracted living somewhere like New York or Chicago. Oklahoma City was perfect because the only thing to do there was play basketball. Play basketball or play Xbox at home and connect online with Dre, who was also a big gamer.

I nearly missed out on playing our first Summer League game because I didn't have insurance. It was all taken care of in the OKC contract, but there was something I hadn't signed yet. The front office rushed the papers to me at the stadium just before the game and I pretty much signed them on the sidelines then ran straight on court. That was my first taste of the business of basketball. I wasn't allowed to play a second of basketball until I had signed that contract in case I got injured and the Thunder lost money on medical expenses or something. To be honest, I didn't really know what I was signing, but I trusted my agents and scribbled my signature on what was put in front of me. I did take a moment to scan the pages and put an interested look on my face, but in fact I had no idea what I was reading. I assume it was all fine since I still have a job.

On the court, everything ran a lot smoother. Summer League is for players who would benefit from more court time. It's usually a mix of rookies and new players yet to start, plus some standouts from the development league squad. Our team was really good and included Reggie Jackson and Jeremy Lamb, who were some of the league's top scorers at the end of the week. I had a solid week, playing four of the five games and holding my own against young centers who had already played a year in the NBA. We won all our games and were crowned Summer League champs, a perfect start to my Thunder career.

Getting to play at that pace for a whole week was good, but what was better was getting coaching from Mark Bryant, or MB, as he's known. He is a former pro player who spent 15 years in the NBA before going straight into coaching. When I joined the Thunder, he was the assistant coach and specifically in charge of the forwards. At 6'9" and twice as wide as me, he wasn't a coach who just gave instructions. He put you through the drills himself. And he was responsible for getting me ready for the big leagues.

Whenever I was subbed out of a game, I made sure to go to the end of the bench so I could sit next to MB and ask him what I could be doing better. Every game he had something for me to work on or try out. I never questioned what he told me because it always seemed to work when I executed it properly. As the years have gone on, MB and I have had our share of disagreements, but we both know that we're on the same team. All it takes is for him to stop what we're doing, look at me for a second, and say, "What are we doing?" He doesn't mean it literally, it's more a "What are we here for?" And it always brings me out of whatever mood I'm in. *What are we doing?* Sometimes all you need to do is ask yourself that when you're in a slump. *What are we doing?* Once you can answer it honestly, your problem is half solved.

By the end of the Summer League, MB was calling me "Big Steve" and the name stuck. I was Big Steve and he was MB. The way he talked to me—not as if I was an idiot but like an adult—and the way he conducted himself, made me like and respect him straight away. I knew that as the bigs coach he would be spending a lot of time with me. He reminded me of Kenny and that told me all I needed to know. I was in safe hands at the Thunder.

12.

SMALL FISH IN A BIG POND

Three days before the start of the 2012–13 season, the Oklahoma City Thunder traded James Harden to the Houston Rockets. In exchange, the Rockets gave the Thunder a whole bunch of players and picks, including the number 12 pick in the 2013 draft. Harden was the reigning sixth man of the year and a huge asset to the team when he got traded, so fans were hoping for a Harden replacement with the draft pick. I'm nothing like James Harden.

I wasn't booed the way some players are, especially those who are drafted by the New York Knicks, but Thunder fans weren't exactly jumping out of their seats with excitement. Fans and media seemed to be in agreement that I wasn't a *bad* draft pick, but I wasn't going to be very helpful for at least a couple of years. Talk of the "D-League" got thrown around a lot when discussing my rookie year. Now known as the G League, it is the NBA's development league that runs alongside the regular season.

Teams will send a player to the G League to work on their game or get some time on the court if management feel they are not ready for the big league just yet. Sometimes players can do both, playing in G League games and NBA games in the same week. Thunder media and fans figured I'd be sent to the Thunder's G League team—then the Tulsa 66ers, now the OKC Blue—for at least my first season because I was "too raw and undeveloped" for the Thunder. I also saw a lot of NBA "experts" popping up in New Zealand saying it was a curse being drafted by a playoff team because it meant I'd be sent to the development league and might never make it back.

I heard all the commentary and I ignored all the commentary. I found out later that the moment I was drafted someone tweeted "WELP STEVEN ADAMS TO OKC" and Kevin Durant apparently replied "smh" ("shaking my head"). He deleted the tweet and replaced it with "Welcome Steven Adams." Not the warmest welcome I'd ever received, but my new teammates' feelings about me weren't my concern. My responsibility was working hard with the coaches to earn my spot on the roster for the regular season. Having MB right there on the bench throughout the Summer League meant I already had a long list of things to work on once I got back to Oklahoma City. But, first, it was back to New Zealand for the northern summer and my first unofficial Steven Adams Camp.

Everyone on the Thunder roster was on summer break and spread out across the country so I had some time to relax. And whenever I have time to relax, I want to go home. I told Mats that I wanted to go home and help out Kenny with his new

OKC TEAM ROSTER 2013–14

STEVEN ADAMS, center

CARON BUTLER, forward

NICK COLLISON, forward

KEVIN "KD" DURANT, forward

DEREK FISHER, guard

SERGE IBAKA, forward

REGGIE JACKSON, guard

GRANT JERRETT, forward

PERRY JONES, forward

JEREMY LAMB, guard

KENDRICK "PERK" PERKINS, center

ANDRE "DRE" ROBERSON, guard

THABO SEFOLOSHA, guard

HASHEEM THABEET, center

RUSSELL "RUSS" WESTBROOK, guard

basketball program, New Zealand Basketball Academy (NZBA), and we came up with the idea of holding a training camp for kids in Wellington. Brook Lopez from the Brooklyn Nets shared the same agent and came along as our guest and all-star coach.

The camp was just the one day at the ASB Sports Centre, but seeing 250 kids so passionate about basketball made it worth the trip. I fell in love with the mentoring side of the game and decided right there that I would grow the camp every year to try to reach as many young players as possible.

While I was back in New Zealand I went to see Mohi and spent a day on the farm. We drove around on quad bikes in the rain feeding the animals. I put up some photos online of our outing and was bombarded with messages saying that the Thunder management would be mad that I was placing myself at risk. It was my first insight into how protective organizations are of their players. Given they are paying us millions of dollars, I suppose the least we can do is not risk falling off a quad bike.

On my way back to Oklahoma I stopped in Portland to do a promo for adidas, who had recently signed me on as an ambassador. Gav met me and we did a presentation for the adidas guys on how we had trained before the draft. I could see they were amazed that they were being taught things about basketball training and injury prevention from some random guy from New Zealand. I was so proud in that moment because it showed that I wasn't just working with a competent trainer, I was working with one of the best in the business.

By the time I had made my way back to Oklahoma City and

settled into my new home, it was time for the Thunder training camp.

It was as hard as any training I had done on the court, but what made it horrific was the same thing that made it more enjoyable than most. That was the mental workout. Yes, I sweated and puffed more than ever—and I was supposedly at my fittest going in—but it was learning all the systems and how to adapt to them that knocked me out. Luckily, I knew that I was pretty much a clean slate and so was ready to soak up everything that anyone said. Some rookies come straight from being a superstar in their college team and have to adjust to being at the bottom of the totem pole. My advantage was that I was comfortable there and I knew how little I knew. There is nothing wrong with being ignorant, as long as you know it and are willing to learn.

It became clear to me that my main influences throughout the season would be MB, Kendrick "Perk" Perkins, and Nick Collison. Nick and Perk had each been in the league for a decade already (Perk had a championship ring too) playing my position, and they knew that I had been brought in to eventually (hopefully) fill their role. Nick seemed happy to guide me through the systems and to try to get me up to speed as fast as possible. Perk? Not so much.

Perk's a big guy and he's tough too. He's not about that friendly banter. MB had been working with me hard out to prepare for training, but with Perk it was still a shock. That guy can throw his weight around. I was used to playing in New Zealand against short rugby players who like to throw themselves at you, but at least I was bigger and could sort them out quite easily. Suddenly, I was the smaller one and here was Perk practically assaulting me every day at practice. It was time to adapt or die, and I wasn't ready to lie down just yet. I started to fight back. If he was going to tug shirts and hold down arms, so was I. He might have been bigger, but I had speed on him and would use that to annoy him. By the end of training camp, I thought I'd made good progress. Perk wasn't pushing me around as much and I was giving as good as I got. Maybe I was giving too much because as we were finishing up a scrimmage we got tangled up off the ball and I *may* have *accidentally* elbowed him. He retaliated by throwing a massive elbow into my ribs, winding me and yelling, "I'm the only silverback!"

I was stunned. I thought I heard some of the other guys laughing, but I was too busy worrying that Perk would keep going and just kill me to save time. I had had scuffles with opponents, but this was a whole new level—and he was on the same team as me. Walking back to the changing rooms to shower, I realized I would have to get a whole lot tougher if I was going to match up against NBA centers throughout the league. As I was packing up to leave the gym for the day, MB wandered by and muttered, "You know silverbacks have the smallest dicks, right?" It cracked me up. I didn't even know if it was true, but it reassured me that I must be doing something right.

I never spoke to Perk about that wee incident again. The next day he came into training and we said hello and got back to smashing each other on the court like usual. Perk was never one to hold grudges. If you annoyed him, he'd tell you, then expect everyone to get back to work. I followed his lead and didn't dwell on it. I figured I'd get much more of the same once the season started so I might as well get used to it. Turns out, the most pain I felt early in that season was when someone pointed out that the Thunder media team had Photoshopped my gold tooth out of my media day headshot like it was a pimple or something. Thankfully, they never did it again.

Looking back, Perk was the best teammate I could've hoped for in my rookie season. I went into training camp playing physical ball because I thought that's what the league would be like. But Perk was even tougher than I expected, and he forced me to quickly up my game. If I had gone to a team without a huge presence at center already, things might have worked out differently. As it happened, I went into our first U.S. preseason game expecting a much more physical game than I got.

It was in fact our third preseason game because we had already played two in Europe against Istanbul and the 76ers, which we won. I didn't really count them, though, since it felt like I was on holiday.

It was also the first home game of the season—playing the Denver Nuggets—and I was nervous. The other guys didn't seem too pumped because preseason games don't count towards a team's final win–loss tally, but those preseason games were my chance to show that I could handle being in the Thunder squad for the regular season. I went out and played as hard as I could, which turned out to be harder than anyone wanted to face during the preseason warm-up games.

The game was going well. We had a commanding lead from the beginning. Perk was resting (remember, it was preseason) so Hasheem Thabeet started in his place. I played 18 minutes and spent most of that time struggling to keep up with the plays. At the start of the fourth quarter, I found myself once again behind on the play, stranded in the middle of the key, with Nick handling the ball at the top of the key. He motioned for me to set an off-ball screen for Derek Fisher, who was on the wing, and I listened. Derek cut sharply to the hoop off my shoulder and Nate Robinson, who was guarding him, followed and ran into me before falling over. Derek ended up with the ball and shot it, so I went to get the rebound, but Robinson was still there. Without thinking I kind of picked him up and moved him to the side so I could get to the basket. I felt a push on my back and then, as I ran back down the court after Derek made the shot, I took another hit on my chest.

It didn't feel like much at all. In fact, I figured it was just someone turning around and nudging me accidentally so I kept running back to position. When I got there and turned around, Robinson was being ejected. I thought he must have yelled at the ref and was sad I missed it. Then I saw on the replay that he got ejected for punching me. So that's what the nudge was.

After the game I asked MB and the guys if I'd done something wrong that made Robinson angry. They laughed and told me to keep doing what I was doing. I did, and went home happy to have helped out the team, albeit in an unconventional way.

The next game, against the New Orleans Pelicans, I was rewarded with more minutes, playing nearly the whole game that ended in a three-point loss. It was my first taste of the endurance required to play at that level and, even at the slower tempo of preseason, I was gassed by the end. But I managed to get a game-high 15 rebounds to show the coaches that when I was given a task, I could complete it efficiently. My task certainly wasn't to score, not with KD on the court.

By the end of preseason, I was feeling a little more comfortable on court and regularly topping the rebounding stats. At this point, nobody had said anything to me about playing in the development league and I wasn't about to bring it up, so I showed up to training every day and as long as no one told me not to, I showed up to the games.

Dre Roberson and I were the two rookies on the roster that season, so were each given a senior player to "assist" on road trips, although we really had to do what everyone said, not just our veteran buddies. Dre was paired up with Perk, and I had Russell Westbrook. You hear stories about the hazing that has happened at other teams—the ritual humiliation of the newbies. There was nothing like that. The Thunder culture is more family than fraternity, so the only form of rookie hazing was just stuff that little brothers would be expected to do for their elders. I carried Russ's bags to the plane and picked him up food on the way if he requested it. Dre got fined a bunch of times for being late to the plane because Perk had ordered food from him. Fines are $750 for a first offense, then $3,000, $5,000, and on and on. I was always on time.

The Thunder plane is amazing. It barely counts as a disadvantage having to travel when you get to fly on a private plane with recliners and tables and a stocked pantry. Once we landed in a city for an away game everyone would go to their own hotel rooms before having a shootaround. I never took my own shampoo or body wash because the hotels would have all that stuff. But almost everyone else in the team was a bit more particular about their grooming, including Russ. Let's just say that I purchased a lot of body wash that season which I never got to use.

I don't remember much about my first ever regular season debut. I know it was against the Utah Jazz because I had a real nice New Zealand steak there that made me like the place. There were a lot more fans than during preseason, but at the same time it didn't feel like a huge occasion because I'd technically already played six games with the Thunder, including one against the Jazz.

We won that first regular-season game and I got my first career points, ending with four points and three rebounds while marking a European center called Enes Kanter. A week later I recorded my first double-double during a win against Detroit, with 17 points and 10 rebounds. I didn't do anything different that game, but after I made my first few shot attempts, Russ kept looking for me inside.

I was looking forward to our second game that same week against the Dallas Mavericks because it meant I could see my old mate Dirk Nowitzki again. He didn't remember me enough to say hi and I didn't want to bother him, but I really felt our friendship grow that day. We won, and I thought that win would be memorable because it marked the first time I got "faded" by Dirk. "Faded" meaning scored on by his signature fadeaway jump shot. Instead it was memorable because I got the legend Vince Carter ejected.

I didn't mean to. I never mean to. I caught an offensive rebound in the low post and Carter was guarding me on my left. As every basketball player is taught to do when playing in the low post, I gripped the ball with two hands and stuck my elbows out for protection while I tried to pivot into space. But Carter is 6′6″ as opposed to my 7-foot self, so my swinging elbow clocked him on the side of the head before I passed back out for a shot. When the shot went up a second later, I tried to get past Carter again for the rebound and was hit on the cheek on my way through. The whistle blew as I caught the rebound and heard Russ yelling, "He can't do that shit, man!"

I looked around and pointed to myself. Was he talking about me? I thought it was a bit late to be calling my elbow, especially since it was accidental. We formed a team huddle while the refs reviewed the play and I watched myself get elbowed in the face by Vince Carter on the huge TV. It looked kinda funny in slow motion, but I couldn't laugh otherwise I'd look bad, so I just watched and chewed my gum and tried to look nonchalant while the crowd booed for my poor cheekbone.

The refs ended up giving me a technical for my first (admittedly uncalled) foul, which was my first real technical ever. I'd had technicals that were defensive three-second violations, which aren't the same thing. As they announced it over the speakers, I thought it was all a bit unfair until they added that Carter got a flagrant 2 technical foul, which meant automatic ejection from the game. As I shot my free throws I wondered if he hated me and really hoped not. After the game I asked MB again if I was doing something wrong and again he said, "No, keep doing what you're doing."

It took two weeks of preseason games and one week of regular-season games for people to stop saying that I'd be spending my rookie year in the development league. I wouldn't have been confident enough to bet money on it, but I definitely didn't feel like I was going anywhere. I'd already exceeded expectations by not being completely out of my depth, and the OKC fans were loving the fact that I was a Kiwi who wasn't dramatic. I knew all along that I had what it took to at least be a bruiser coming off the bench, but even I didn't think I'd be starting within two weeks of the season opener.

Perk's grandfather passed away the day before we were leaving for a series of away games on the West Coast. He couldn't make at least two games, so suddenly there was an opening in the starting five for a center. I thought the coach, Scott (Scotty) Brooks, would start Nick, but when he named the starting five that day in Los Angeles, there I was. And there's nothing like matching up against DeAndre Jordan for your first starting appearance. I was almost glad it was an away game. The Thunder crowd are so loyal and supportive that they would have loved cheering me on, which would have made me nervous about not letting them down. The LA Clippers fans at the Staples Center in Los Angeles didn't give two shits that it was a big moment for me. In the end I had a quiet game because DeAndre Jordan is a big man who knows how to dominate the key.

Once the season gets going, all the games start to merge into one. Life becomes a blur of flights, hotels, and endless different basketball courts. Players generally remember games specifically because they were really good or they were really bad. I was lucky enough not to have any truly bad games in 2013, the first half of the season. I got Jordan Hamilton of the Nuggets ejected for perhaps the softest flagrant foul in NBA history (which is saying something). He was running on transition and I slowed down to get in his way. When he ran into me, he swung his arm out instinctively and hit me about as hard as a toddler hits their parent. Because of his intent (to hurt me, I guess) he was ejected and suspended for a game. Other than that incident, the last months of the year were filled with steady progress and gradual stat improvement, which was exactly what I was working towards.

While my friends back in New Zealand were celebrating the first days of 2014 by getting drunk and passing out in paddocks, I marked the occasion by fouling out in three consecutive games. My first foul-out was against the Houston Rockets, matching up against Dwight Howard, the guy with the bubble arms. I came in off the bench and went straight to fouling. A lot of the time when you get called for a foul, you know you've fouled. Even if you look all shocked and like that shrugging emoji, you know you kinda deserved it. The difference in my rookie season is that I got called for *a lot* of fouls that I genuinely didn't know were fouls.

Early in the fourth quarter, when I was sitting on five fouls, Dwight (who was on four fouls himself) and I got into it off the ball and were called for a double foul. Dwight was subbed off with five fouls and I was fouled out for the first time with six. There's a funny GIF out there somewhere of us reacting in unison to the ref's call, but that's really the only good thing to come out of that game.

I managed to foul out in 10 minutes of playing time, which has got to be some sort of record. What it definitely was on the night was embarrassing. Fouling out always stinks because it means you're useless to your team and have to watch the rest of the game from the bench. Fouling out after starting on the bench is worse as it means you were supposed to be giving an energy boost and letting the starters rest, and instead you put yourself out of the game. Fouling out after starting on the bench and playing only 10 minutes is beyond stink. I pledged that day that I would never do it again.

The very next day we played the Golden State Warriors at home—and what did I do? I fouled out after starting on the bench and playing only 10 minutes. It might seem funny now, but trust me, it wasn't funny when it happened. This time I managed to not foul until the final minutes of the first quarter, which was a fairly rare feat for me my whole rookie season. But with three fouls before halftime, it was feeling a bit like déjà vu. Cut to the fourth quarter and I picked up my fifth foul. Before coach could even think about pulling me out, the ball went back down the court, Klay Thompson scored, and we were back on offense, which I thought was a safer area for me foul-wise. On that play, I set up in the low post, pivoted, and was called for a charge. Six fouls, back on the bench.

We had a rest the next day, so I could think about my 12 fouls in 48 hours, and then we were back at the arena playing DeMarcus Cousins and the Sacramento Kings. Cousins is easily one of the toughest guys to mark in the league. He's strong but also plays angry, so you never know what he might suddenly do. I can take a punch to the face better than anyone, but even I would like a bit of warning. I wasn't looking forward to playing him because he was physical, and when you match up with an enforcer, you can't help but dial up your own roughness. That almost always means more fouls for everyone.

As it turned out, I didn't get my first foul until five minutes into the second quarter, but I also wasn't getting anything else. My shot was off, and my confidence was low after the previous two games. I was doing a good job of making sure every Cousins shot was a contested one, but I was still fouling and was fouled out for the third time in a row with five minutes left to play.

Fouling out in three consecutive games made me question my whole style of play. It wasn't just one end of the floor either; I was getting called for shooting fouls, offensive fouls, loose ball fouls. I started to wonder whether the refs had had a talk and decided that all the things I was doing to piss off other guys and get them ejected would now be fouls. If that was the case, I was screwed. I spoke to Scotty after that third game and asked him if I should maybe try being a bit less physical so I could stop getting fouled out all the time. He didn't hesitate at all in telling me no. In fact, he said the only reason he'd get angry was if I changed how I played.

Turns out refs are just like players and need to study how teams play before every game so they know how best to officiate. When a bunch of rookies come in each season, refs don't know how they play and it can take a while for them to get used to the new players' styles. I was big and staunch, so when refs saw veterans ending up on the floor after running into me, of course they were going to call a foul on the big rookie. Nowadays, those same plays wouldn't be called as fouls against me because those same refs now know how I play.

But, at the time, I didn't know what to do. I thought I'd keep getting calls against me and fouling out every game until I was forced to retire. It's something almost every rookie who gets decent playing time has to go through, and as the years went by I saw it happening to new guys every season. There's nothing anyone else can do but continue to encourage them and empathize. Nobody told me to do anything differently because they all knew it would pass, and it did. I didn't foul out the rest of my rookie season.

The next few games I tried to play like normal, but it's impossible to not adjust at least a little bit after fouling out so quickly three games in a row. Thankfully, it didn't take long before I was back annoying opponents and catching elbows. My last ejection of that season had happened a few days before my terrible fouling spree, against the Milwaukee Bucks.

Once again it was a scuffle that happened off the ball. In the middle of the second quarter, Reggie Jackson set up on the wing for a three-point shot while I cut to the basket, ready for the rebound. On my way in I bumped Larry Sanders. It was an intentional bump because no big ever cuts through the paint without making contact with anyone. So I bumped him and he bumped me back and it was all fun bumping, until he decided to bump me in the throat with his forearm. He was ejected and later fined $2,000.

I didn't understand how all these players could react so aggressively to me all the time. I figured they must all have grown up as only children. Anyone who grew up with a bunch of siblings knows that parents are basically just refs for the first 10 years of your life. The trick was to annoy your siblings as much as you could without being caught by your household ref. Nudge them, bump them, stand in their way, but insist you're not touching them. These are all little kiddie moves that work just as well on the basketball court. At home, if you cracked first and tried to punch your sibling in front of your parents, everyone got a hiding. But on the basketball court, if you lose your cool first, you're usually the only one who gets punished.

I grew up the youngest of 14 kids. My ability to annoy and my capacity to withstand physical taunts is pretty bloody high. I think what took those veterans by surprise was that I was a mere rookie and yet had the gall to annoy them and make them crack. I think some of them considered it disrespectful of me or some sort of dirty tactic. No, it was just that in that particular aspect of the game I'd had a lifetime of practice. When I started in the NBA I was already a veteran in taking hits.

13.

SMALL FISH IN A BIGGER POND

In my first NBA season, I found myself taking the court in the playoffs. We had finished second in the Western Conference behind the San Antonio Spurs and were well positioned for a strong playoff run. Our first best-of-seven playoff series would be against the seventh-place Memphis Grizzlies. In theory, this should be the easiest series in a playoff run, but in the NBA there's no such thing as an easy series. Every team plays differently and so every team requires the same diligent approach.

Not everyone gets to experience the playoffs in their rookie season. Some players don't get to experience it their whole career. I was just lucky that I got drafted by such a good team.

The playoffs really are something else. Regular season is fun, but by the time you get to game 70 of 82, you're ready for it to be over. Once the playoffs start, you might as well throw your whole regular season out the window because it means nothing now. All that matters is winning four games against one team.

And then winning four more against another. Repeat, until you're NBA Champions.

Preparing for a playoff series is like studying for an exam. During the regular season there are so many games that teams only get a few hours to think about their opponents' systems and how they like to play. But in the playoffs, the week before that first game is spent going over hours and hours of footage, figuring out what your opponent likes to do and then working out how to force them to do anything but that. If they like to pick-and-roll for 90 percent of the time and play in isolation for 10 percent, you figure out how to make them play in isolation the whole time. It's all mental work and is so much tougher than physically playing a game.

After we'd done our film work, the bigs and the guards separated to each study our match-ups in the Grizzlies and suss out how they played individually and what, if any, were their weaknesses. Perk and I were studying Marc Gasol and Zach Randolph. Gasol was an idol of mine as a big man who was agile and could shoot outside the paint, and Randolph was a tank of a man with aggression to rival DeMarcus Cousins. We knew that the Grizzlies liked to slow the game down and force teams to play at their pace, so our approach was to try to outrun them and speed everything up. This meant that even though it was my first playoffs, I'd probably be seeing a bit of court time.

Being the higher seed, we were given home-court advantage for the first two games and I got to see the transformation that happens in Oklahoma City when the playoffs start. Every home game sold out in minutes and the noise inside the Chesapeake Arena never stopped. I could barely hear my own teammates calling for the ball. It made me realize how quiet Kiwi fans are at pretty much every New Zealand sporting event.

We started the game doing exactly what we planned to do—run transition and not let them control the pace—and it worked incredibly well. Thanks to our natural hustle defense and fast transitions, we were up by 22 points at halftime. But as every NBA fan knows, there's no such thing as a safe halftime lead. The Grizzlies came back out a new team and suddenly it was them controlling the pace by slowing things down and shutting down our fast breaks. By the end of the third quarter, our lead had been cut to nine.

The small-ball approach was working though, so Perk and I spent most of the game on the bench while Serge Ibaka and Caron Butler played as power forwards without a center. We got our groove back in the fourth quarter and finished with 100–86 to take a 1–0 lead in the series. It was a typically fast game. In the playoffs every quarter is played like the final minutes of a close regular-season game. By that point, though, everyone is so fit that the physical demands of the playoffs are hardly a factor. It's the extra mental work that leaves you drained.

If preparing for the playoffs is like studying for an exam, playing the actual series is like a boxing match. The first game in the series is like the first round. Everyone's playing hard, but you're really just dancing around each other, throwing jabs and trying to figure out what everyone's moves are.

After that first game we went away and watched footage to see what we had missed in our preparations and what adjustments we needed to make for game two. Because our fast, small

OWHATA PRIMARY SCHOOL
Room 16, New Entrants - 1998

Teacher: Mrs Maureen Head

ABOVE: First year of school, the tallest one at the back. I look cute but I definitely wasn't the teacher's pet.
Adams family collection

RIGHT: Must've been about 11 in this photo. Even back then I knew my nuts would take a hiding some day.
Adams family collection

TOP: The youngest 'lot' of Adams kids. L–R: me, Dad, Gabby, Lisa, and Sid. *Adams family collection*

BOTTOM: Me and my old man. It's a cheesy photo but pretty much shows exactly how I felt about him. *New Zealand Herald / newspix.co.nz*

TOP: The infamous Adams family photo. L–R: Warren, Rob, Barry, Ralph, Sid, Dad, Val, Lisa, Mohi, Paddy, Les, Gabby, Viv, Margaret. Next to Margaret and not in shot: me. Note the rugged basketball hoop in the background where I first learned the game. *Adams family collection*

BOTTOM: With Blossom at the College Sport Wellington awards in 2011. *Scots College archive*

ABOVE: National champions, with Debbie Webb (far left), Bernice Williams, Chris (13), Victor (12), Jah Wee (6), and Joseph (8). *Webb family collection*

LEFT: Scots College did a lot for me and in return I gave them a pretty good poster boy. *Stuff / Dominion Post*

RIGHT: Kenny and me, a team from the very beginning. *Kenny McFadden collection*

ABOVE: I spent more time with my Wellington teammates than anyone else. When we weren't working on the court we were working off it to fundraise for our tournaments. *Webb family collection*

ABOVE AND LEFT: Mohi's farm has always been my favorite place to relax, as much as it makes the Thunder management nervous. *Adams family collection*

RIGHT: Being in the Wellington Saints was my first experience playing against grown men who could push me around. *Hagen Hopkins / Getty Images*

TOP: Working hard at Pitt. My toughest year of basketball to date. *Fred Vuich / Sports Illustrated / Getty Images*

BOTTOM: L–R: Kenny, Sid, me, and Mohi having a pre-draft breakfast and feeling suffocated in our shirts and ties. *Adams family collection*

RIGHT: Scrubbing up nice for the draft and always repping New Zealand hard. My head was too big for that hat. *Jesse D. Garrabrant / NBAE via Getty Images*

PREVIOUS SPREAD: One of the first Steven Adams camps. They get bigger and bigger every year. *Hagen Hopkins / Getty Images*

LEFT: In my rookie year I spent most of my time trying to do exactly what the coaches had told me to do and nothing else besides block shots. *Greg Nelson / Sports Illustrated / Getty Images*

TOP: It was an honor every single time I got to step onto the court with Tim Duncan. And it was an honor every single time he slapped me in the face while I tried to dunk.
Layne Murdoch Jr. / NBAE via Getty Images

BOTTOM: I love visiting these ladies at home and beating them at their own game. *Zach Beeker / NBAE via Getty Images*

TOP: Ain't nothing wrong with a bunch of tissue stuffed up your nose if it means you can get back out on the court. *John W. McDonough / Sports Illustrated / Getty Images*

BOTTOM: We had planned to win the championship in 2016 with this team, but things don't often go to plan. *Greg Nelson / Sports Illustrated / Getty Images*

RIGHT: This is probably the closest I got to a Tom Selleck mustache, which is more satisfying than the dunk. *Layne Murdoch / NBAE via Getty Images*

2013

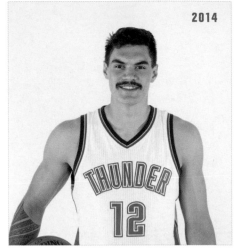

2014

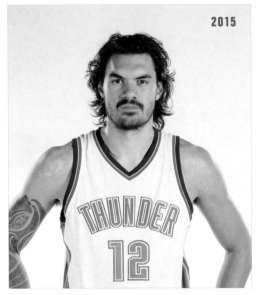

2015

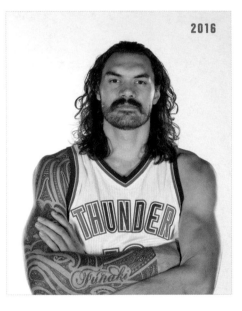

2016

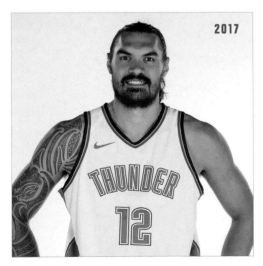

2017

THIS PAGE: I've changed a bit in five years and learned a lot. Still haven't learned how to smile properly though. *Layne Murdoch / NBAE via Getty Images, except top right Richard Rowe / NBAE via Getty Images*

game had worked so well, our only adjustment was to focus on not lagging after halftime.

Game two turned out to be one of the best games in the whole of the 2013 NBA playoffs. I played two minutes and spent the rest of the game as on edge as the 18,000-strong crowd. With 18.1 seconds to go in regulation time, the Grizzlies were up 98–93, but we had possession. Russ tried to pass to Kevin "KD" Durant for a corner three, but it got deflected.

When the ball is loose in a game, it's like everything stops. Every player on the court has to make a split-second decision whether to go for the ball or leave it. A moment's hesitation and you're out, mate. Our Thunder practices had everyone diving on every loose ball, even in the scrimmages, which set us up to be one of the best defending teams for deflections and loose ball recoveries. That night against the Grizzlies it came in handy.

Russ scrambled to retrieve the loose ball, scooped it up, and threw it to KD who was already falling out-of-bounds after being fouled. He shot it as he fell onto someone's lap and it somehow went in. It was ridiculous. He made the free throw and the score was suddenly 98–97 with 13.8 on the clock. We fouled down the other end to stop the clock and the Grizzlies made one free throw: 99–97. With one second on the clock, Russ shot a tough three, which missed. But Perk, the steady ship, was under the hoop and managed to tap it in just as the buzzer sounded: 99–99. I'd never heard anything as loud as the cheer that erupted when that ball rolled through the net.

Sadly, in a major anti-climax, the Grizzlies ended up winning in overtime, 111–105. It was devastating, not just to lose but to lose at home too. Everyone wants to win a series 4–0 to get as long a rest as possible before the next round, but now we'd be playing at least five games, with the next two in Memphis.

Games three, four, and five all went into overtime—not your usual first-round playoff series. The Grizzlies took game three, we took game four, and the Grizzlies took game five. I didn't play in games three or five, and I was in for just five minutes in game four. But I was ready to go as soon as my team needed me. Down 3–2 in the series, game six was obviously a must-win. And that's when I was able to make my accidental trademark move of having someone punch me.

I got in for 20 minutes and made sure it counted. They didn't need my help scoring and I wasn't getting a bunch of rebounds so I just made sure no one would score on me. I had been resting on the bench for a week and my legs felt springy, so I went out and got a then career-high five blocks. In the middle of the fourth quarter, I turned around on transition to run my lane and ended up tangled with Zach Randolph. I pulled my arm away and I guess he didn't like how I did it because he shoved me. I was so exhausted by this point that when he shoved me I didn't have the energy to correct my course, so I just kept jogging in the direction he pushed me to avoid falling over. The refs called a common foul and I got told off by Russ for not calling a screen that had blindsided him the play before. We won the game by 20 points.

After the game, the foul was reviewed and the NBA suspended Randolph for one game, meaning he would miss the game seven decider. It was back at home, where we won 120–109. I almost felt bad about Randolph's suspension because I knew he'd have been beating himself up over being unavailable for game seven. He was an impact player for the Grizzlies and his absence made all the difference. I wouldn't have been surprised if he had held a grudge over it for years, but the first time I matched up against him the next season, we were all good.

In the second round of the playoffs, our series against the Clippers wasn't harder than the Grizzlies, just different. The Clippers played a similar game to us, with fast transitions. But, at the same time, they had DeAndre Jordan and Glen "Big Baby" Davis on the inside so their big game was strong.

Commentators like to say a series gets interesting once a team loses at home. We had home advantage again and lost the first game 122–105, so I guess the series was interesting from the start. It was the first game and Chris Paul shot 85 percent from the field. When someone is on fire like that, there really isn't much you can do. We took the loss and regrouped for game two. With our second home game, and a good kick up the arse, we won an up-and-down game 112–101.

Heading back to Staples Center in Los Angeles, where I had had my first start, we carried our momentum with us and won game three 118–112. KD had been top-scoring most games with at least 30 points, but Russ was always right there. In game three, I got a few more minutes and was able to bring down a team-high nine rebounds. Leading 2–1 and coming off an away win, we had all the momentum going into game four. Unfortunately, we took all that momentum and turned it into quite an impressive choke.

Nine minutes into the game we were up 29–7. The Clippers were shooting well below 50 percent, while it felt like we couldn't miss. The first thing that happened to me when I was subbed in at the end of the first quarter was I nearly got knocked out by Glen Davis on an attempted dunk. I saw stars for a second but was otherwise fine. I'll still happily blame the hit for my two missed free throws, though. In six minutes of play I was called for three fouls, but there were fouls being called for everything as tensions ran high. Davis and I were going at it. Blake Griffin was getting pissed at me for trying to get rebounds. I wanted to stay in. I felt like I was in the middle of a fight that I had to finish. But it wasn't even halftime, and three fouls is three fouls. So I was out and back on the bench as the Clippers cut our lead to four.

Starting the second half with a 10-point lead was handy but clearly not enough to get comfortable, especially when the lead had been 22. The game was one of the most physical of the season and I was sitting on the bench, itching to get back in and hustle. Near the end of the third quarter, I got my chance and went straight to work trying to make Jordan ineffective. We went into the fourth quarter up by 12 and shooting way better than them. People should have been safe betting on us to win after three quarters leading consistently. And those same people would have lost their money.

I was doing well to battle Jordan for every ball, but after two soft foul calls early in the fourth I was back on the bench with five fouls, frustrated. At that point there were eight minutes to go in the game and we were up by 12 again.

With 1 minute and 23 seconds on the clock, the Clippers took the lead for the first time. They held the lead for just 75 seconds the entire game, but they were the only 75 seconds that mattered. After leading by 22 points in the first quarter, we lost 101–99.

We won game five by one point in the final moments, but it will probably be remembered only for a controversial last minute of officiating from the refs. We were trailing by seven points with 49 seconds remaining and ended up winning the game, which basically every Clippers fan thought was thanks to some unfair calls going our way. The Clippers coach, Doc Rivers, didn't even try to hide his anger after the game and ended up getting fined for criticizing the refs.

All I'll say is KD still had to make a clutch three for us to win that game. We still had to make a steal and get a fast break layup to win that game. And Russ still had to make three ridiculous pressure free throws to take the lead and win that game. As for the controversial out-of-bounds call given to us that everyone says went off our guy Reggie Jackson's hand? I couldn't possibly comment. Reggie was in a three-on-one fast break situation and chose to take it himself instead of passing to KD or Russ. That's far more controversial to me.

Perk got into foul trouble early in the first quarter of game six and I was in earlier than planned. It didn't start well. I'd been working hard on having soft hands and not fumbling passes and rebounds, but I fumbled two almost immediately. I tried to throw the ball off Chris Paul and out-of-bounds, but he caught it. Then he did the exact same thing to me and I couldn't catch it. The only thing that wasn't frustrating me was my shooting, which was safe. I led the team in scoring in the first quarter. But that changed quickly once KD got going.

We still trailed for the whole of the first half, sometimes by as many as 16 points. We'd make a run and get back to within five and then take our foot off the pedal for a minute and suddenly we were down by 15 again. Playing catch-up for two quarters drains you. But then Nick came on court and everything turned around.

When a team plays for long enough, they develop a sixth sense of each other on the court. During my rookie season, I hadn't gotten to the point of knowing where everyone was all the time, but fairly quickly I developed a shorthand with Nick and Perk. When any two of us were on the court together, we knew what to do.

Nick subbed in and we got straight to work shutting down the Clippers' scoring and trimming their 15-point lead. Nick was getting charges and I was getting blocks. We were always in the right spots at the right time. I'd gamble on defense, knowing he had my back, and then he would do the same and I'd have his back. Knowing that you can afford to play aggressive defense because your teammate is covering for you makes all the difference to getting stops. Nick and I did that, and they just couldn't score. It shut them down completely.

Then, going into the final quarter, I got a defensive rebound, sent it down the court where Nick had planted up in the corner, and he sank a three right on the buzzer to draw the game. The Clippers had led the entire game up to that point and never led again. We won the game 104–98 and the series 4–2. We were going to the Western Conference finals.

That game became mine and Nick's claim to fame. His because of that crucial shot and mine because I played 40 minutes, the longest I'd ever played in any NBA game, let alone a playoff match. I'd never been as exhausted on the court as I was in the final quarter of that game. But even though I felt like I was dying, it was mean because I knew I was making a very real and sustained impact for my team. Doing some good stuff in a few minutes off the bench was cool, but playing nearly the entire game in a huge win was something else. We talk about that game even now to all the young fellas.

The San Antonio Spurs had won their Western Conference semifinals 4–1, so they had an extra day of rest before the first game of our series. Going into game 96 of the season, that extra 24 hours helps the body recover a lot. But where it makes all the difference is in having more time to study your opponent. We needed two weeks to strategize for the 2013/14 Spurs, not two days.

Every single playoff team believes they can win the championship. If you don't expect to be the best, you shouldn't be playing in the NBA. While we fully intended to win both the conference finals and the championship finals, Serge had just been ruled out of the first game with a calf injury and the Spurs were the clear favorites to take out both the series and the championship.

Their team was...I don't even know. It was almost stupid. They were playing a different game from everyone else. The whole squad was old, but in a good way. Kawhi Leonard was pretty much their youngest player and he's two years older than me. Playing against the Spurs in 2014 was like playing against a team who had been together for a decade, which for their big three—Tim Duncan, Manu Ginobili, and Tony Parker—was actually true. I love all those guys because they just seem like really chill, nice guys and playing against them in the conference finals was the closest I ever got to buzzing out in an NBA game. Not to mention they had my idol Pop for a coach and legendary Kiwi Sean Marks as assistant coach.

If you don't know who Sean Marks is, do yourself a favor and look him up. Sean was the first New Zealand–born player to ever play in the NBA after being drafted forty-fourth by the New York Knicks in 1998. He played 11 seasons in the NBA and averaged 2.8 points per game. They don't let just anyone averaging two points per game stick around in the league that long. Clearly, he was bringing something else to the table, and that was his brains. As soon as Sean retired, he joined the Spurs' front office as an assistant in basketball operations, before becoming assistant coach for three seasons, then assistant general manager. He is now the general manager for the Brooklyn Nets. That sort of career trajectory is legendary and something I aim for.

I never thought I'd be some sort of superstar in the league, I just wanted to have a job in basketball for as long as possible. Most people would have no idea who Sean Marks is and yet he's been in the league for 20 years and has two championship rings, one as a player and one as a coach. That's some dream shit right there.

It was the first series opener we didn't have home advantage for, and it showed. The Thunder franchise had never won an away first game before, and we didn't change history that night, losing convincingly 122–105. The Spurs were just unstoppable. We were a good defensive team, but they had never been like any other team to defend against. Most teams have one, maybe two guys who are their stars and will take most of their shots. It's quite straightforward defending against them because you just worry about shutting that one guy down. If someone is having a great game and shooting 80 percent, you just worry about him. Only having to be aware of one player means that everyone has time to set themselves up on defense and be in the right position to fast break as soon as that shot is taken.

The Spurs weren't like that. They had so much movement and rotation both on and off the ball that it forced defenders to switch constantly. Switching is fine if you can switch back. But when the ball is constantly moving, it's hard to get back into your defensive positions without creating a gap to score through. And that's how you end up with guards trying to box out bigs and being out of position for a fast break. Teams can stuff up their opponent's offensive systems by confusing their defense, and the Spurs were the masters of ruining a defensive system.

"Timmy D" Duncan put on a masterclass of a big-man game. When I subbed in for my short stint on the court, I expected Playoff Timmy to not be as nice as Regular Season Timmy and I was ready to have a physical fight the whole time, like I'd had first with Randolph and then with Jordan. I even figured I just might be able to get an edge on him since I was 20 and he was 38. Surely, I could use my size and speed to shut him down. But that's the thing with legends. They don't need to be the fastest or the strongest. Timmy (I call him Timmy cos apparently that's what his friends call him) knew *exactly* where to be and how to plant and what angles to use to make my size and strength ineffective. You can't shut someone down if you have no idea what they're doing.

Even his trash talk was amazing. Amazing because there was none of it. I was ready for some veteran, aged-like-fine-wine insults. Instead he looked at me and asked how I was doing and said something about it being my first playoffs. I was shocked and didn't really know how to respond to such a nice guy. Then he turned around and scored 27 points on us. To be honest, I would have preferred it if he had just punched me in the face.

If game one was bad, game two was worse. It was in San Antonio again and we just couldn't get into a groove on their home turf. The Spurs adjusted by shutting down KD and Russ, who were both averaging over 30 points per game. In game two they each scored 15 and no one else was able to step up and take over the scoring. We lost 112–77, one of the biggest playoff wins for the Spurs in franchise history. I felt like I'd done better marking Duncan and keeping him to just 14 points, but it didn't really matter when Danny Green shot seven three-pointers. It's hard to stop that sort of fire.

We got Serge back for game three and he made sure everyone knew it by scoring six of our first eight points and bringing everybody up with him. Having Serge back and finally being back home at Chesapeake Arena made all the difference and we got our first win of the series, 106–97.

In game four I dunked on Tim Duncan. That's all that matters. Well, actually, us winning that game was way more important, but for all my mates back home in New Zealand, me dunking on Tim Duncan was all they cared about. I was still building up my confidence to try dunking on anyone and I don't think I would have dared to go up against Duncan like that—it was more luck than anything. I got a pass in the low post and thought I had a clear lane to the basket so I jumped up for the dunk. Duncan, being as sneaky as he is, appeared out of nowhere to contest it and, because I was already well on my way, I went right by him and got the two points. It was a bit more dunking next to him than dunking *on* him, but I'll take it.

Game four was ours too. It's hard to overstate how much of a boost you get from playing in front of a home crowd, but it's honestly massive, especially in the middle of the country where people live and breathe through their sports teams. The Spurs and Thunder have similar diehard fan bases so we knew how hard it was playing in front of each other's crowds.

Bringing the series back to 2–2 we realized that when we could keep Duncan from controlling the game, we had much better chances of winning. And that meant a lot of work for me.

Duncan top-scored in game five and the Spurs embarrassed us in front of their home crowd, 117–89. We stayed in the game until halftime, when we just crashed and ended up missing all our three-point attempts after that and shooting badly in the paint too. It's probably worth noting that while we had three players score in double figures that game, the Spurs had six. That's just what happens when you have players like Ginobili coming off the bench.

At one point during the game I glanced over at the Spurs bench to see Duncan and Sean Marks talking and laughing with each other. Two of my heroes sharing a joke just a few meters away from me. I almost asked them what was so funny, but I didn't want it to be weird.

We flew home that night one loss away from elimination but still confident that we could force a game seven, because every game up to that point had been won by the home team. Game six was in OKC.

Neither team led by more than 10 points the whole game, which is about as close a game as you can get in the NBA. We held the lead throughout most of the first half, but Boris Diaw and Ginobili came off the bench for the Spurs and absolutely smashed it. They pulled ahead, held their lead, and looked all but through. Then with seconds to go we found a way to tie the scores, sending the game into overtime.

In the middle of overtime, while we were all chewing our warm-up tops to shreds on the bench, I suddenly realized I had a front-row seat to one of the great basketball spectacles. I was seeing icons from two different eras of the NBA going up against each other. There were completely different styles of play and yet it was such a close match-up. The privilege of being part of that wasn't lost on me. With five seconds to go in overtime and us down by five, the starting five were subbed out and I went in for the final play of my rookie season.

Our bench scored only five points in the entire game, and all five of those points were by the veteran Derek Fisher. Want to guess how many points the Spurs' bench scored? Fifty-one. Five players—four starters and Derek—scored points for our team while 10 players got on the board for the Spurs. That's every single player except one. Those two stats on their own pretty much sum up the game and the series. Russ and KD could win a lot of games on their own, and they had done so all season. But when you face a team with a bench so strong they can almost outscore the starters, it's just too much. Our two superstars needed their bench to help them and we didn't, not that night. It's a testament to how incredible KD and Russ were that we almost won that game despite everything. We lost 112–107 and the Spurs went on to beat the Miami Heat 4–1 to become the 2014 NBA Champions.

The one tiny good thing to come out of that night was that I got to hug Pop. Only at the end of a playoff series do teams get to shake hands and talk to each other. I learned this the hard way in one of the first games of the season against the Clippers (always the Clippers!) when I tried to shake Byron Mullens' hand and he just walked away. The only thing worse than being left hanging is being left hanging on national TV. So I shook my own hand and made a note to never try that again.

Being knocked out of the finals was heartbreaking, but at the same time I was a rookie who had been able to play *a lot* in an amazing playoff run with one of the best teams in the league. I wasn't exactly sulking. As we went through and said good luck to all the Spurs guys for their final series rematch against the Heat, I dialed in on Pop and made sure he didn't leave before I could embrace him. When I finally got my arms around him... mate, it was beautiful. I just held that legendary man and got a quick sniff of his hair. He smelled lovely. Don't act like you wouldn't do exactly the same thing if you had the chance.

As I made my way off the court I spotted Derek Fisher looking around with a devastated look on his face. After 18 seasons in the league, he'd decided that one was going to be his last. We had all planned to send him out with another ring, but we fell short. As he looked around, the home crowd kept cheering and showing the love they'd shown us all season. I watched him for a little bit and wondered if I'd be able to have such a long, incredible career. Eighteen seasons, five championships with the Lakers, all-time leader in playoff games played, and a crucial member of our team both on and off the court in his final season. He'd taught me so much about how to survive in the NBA, and if I last half as long as him, I'll be happy.

Derek waved goodbye to the crowd for the last time as a professional basketball player while I walked out of the stadium knowing I was just getting started.

14.

INJURIES ARE A BITCH

In the 2014 off-season I had some serious work to do—and I knew my reputation was at stake. I decided to grow a mustache. I was hesitant at first, because if you can't grow a mustache like Tom Selleck then why even bother, but I was getting sick of my rookie look. I waited until the off-season because no way was I going to be seen on TV during a game with some wispy mo'. That would have been serving up insults to my opponents on a silver platter. The off-season gave me two months to work on that thing before presenting it to the world.

The usual rule for rookies is that they have to stick around for most of the summer and continue working on their game so the coaches can keep an eye on them if needed. Thankfully, Gav had come over and observed some of my trainings throughout the season and talked to the coaches. They trusted him to keep me in shape in New Zealand. If the Thunder management didn't trust Gav and Kenny, they wouldn't have let me come back home for more than two weeks tops. Instead I flew home before the Heat and Spurs had even started their final series and went back only for a few weeks to train a little and compete in the Orlando Summer League. Otherwise, I was in Wellington and free as a bird. Or at least as free as a bird that had strict instructions not to get fat.

Growing a mustache was a very real part of my off-season training, even if it wasn't explicitly stated. My rookie season had been spent innocently pissing off veterans and getting under their skin by feigning ignorance. But that only works for so long and we all knew that I wouldn't be able to get away with it for another whole season. Which meant I had to toughen up.

What also helped—although this wasn't the reason I got it— was a new sleeve tattoo from local Wellington artist Tuigamala Andy Tauafiafi. I already had "Funaki," my middle name, tattooed on my right forearm, but it looked lonely there, so I got the rest of the arm filled in up to the elbow with Tongan and Māori designs. It was a good way to mark the end of the beginning of my NBA journey, and I was excited to be able to showcase part of my culture on American TV once the new season started. I wanted both Tongan and Māori designs because those are the cultures I felt closest to. In reality I'm not Māori at all, but I feel like I am. My mum might be Tongan, but because she wasn't around, her kids never really experienced much of the Tongan culture. Dad was British so besides saying some words funny, there wasn't a lot of culture on that side either. It was growing up with Viv and her family that made me feel Māori. Viv's mum was Māori and so is her husband; that's the culture we were raised in.

OKC TEAM ROSTER 2014–15

STEVEN ADAMS, center

D. J. AUGUSTIN, guard

NICK COLLISON, forward

KEVIN "KD" DURANT, forward

SERGE IBAKA, forward

PERRY JONES, forward

ENES KANTER, center

JEREMY LAMB, guard

MITCH MCGARY, center

ANTHONY MORROW, guard

STEVE NOVAK, forward

ANDRE "DRE" ROBERSON, guard

KYLE SINGLER, forward

DION WAITERS, guard

RUSSELL "RUSS" WESTBROOK, guard

I don't have Māori blood, but in New Zealand you don't need that to respect and love the culture of our country.

In August I held my second annual Steven Adams Camp, and this time I brought some of the Thunder. It was a coaching camp so the first person I thought to ask was MB, since he was the coach I worked closest with in OKC. He didn't even pause before saying he'd love to come. Once word got around the organization that I was holding camps in New Zealand and taking MB, the general manager, Sam Presti, asked if he could come along. I said yes because he was the GM and my boss, but I was nervous that he would find something wrong with how I was spending my off-season and shut it down.

After one season as a rookie it would have been really easy, and frankly quite normal, for me to completely separate my life in Oklahoma City from my life in New Zealand. Most players do it. They live and breathe their team during the season, but once that last game is played, they're off on a boat or in Europe and leaving it all behind. After all, playing basketball was my job and people always say not to take your work home with you.

But OKC don't roll like that. Being in the Thunder wasn't just being in a cool workplace, it was being a part of a family who genuinely cared about you and had your best interests at heart, on and off the court. I'd spent the past 12 months going on about how New Zealand had better food than America and better landscapes and better everything, so I wanted to show everyone what they were missing out on.

But at the same time I was nervous, in the way that people get nervous when they introduce their girlfriend to their family. What if MB or Sam said something bad or disrespected the

Māori customs? I wanted to show them the beauty of Māori culture, but I also knew that America doesn't celebrate their indigenous culture in the same way, so maybe they would think it was silly. On the other hand, I was worried that something would go wrong during the trip and give them a bad impression of my home, which they would take back and share with the rest of the Thunder guys. Mate, I was stressing out.

Turns out, it couldn't have gone better. I briefed MB and Sam *a lot* about the traditional Māori pōwhiri welcome that we would receive before each camp, how to hongi, and when to just sit quietly and listen. They might have been my coach and my boss, but in New Zealand I was the expert and they were my students. I explained the respect required for the haka and what it means when one is performed before you, and they listened. And when the haka was performed by the kids at the camps, they listened. There aren't many moments when I've felt as proud to be a Kiwi as seeing my country and culture presented in all its wonder to my NBA family. I knew then that I'd do whatever it took to bring every last one of my teammates to New Zealand to show them where I come from and why I am the way I am. Bringing Sam along to that first camp proved to him (I think) why OKC was the perfect fit for me. The tight-knit community and the focus on doing things without drama fits right in with my New Zealand habits. Once he saw that, I think he understood how I was able to slot into the Thunder system so seamlessly.

I'd naturally gotten stronger in the legs throughout the season—108 games will do that—so the off-season was for making sure those gains weren't lost and to work on evening out the muscle by building a little on my arms and a lot on my core. Gav had been given parameters but other than that it was up to the two of us and Kenny to make sure that I returned to Oklahoma in two months an improved player. I learned quickly that coming back after the off-season fitter than you were at the end of the last season is basically impossible. No training, no matter how hard or competitive, can replicate the intensity of a game situation. But the point is you have to at least *try* to maintain some fitness so there's not too much to make up once you get back to training camp in the preseason. Then MB asks if you kept in shape and you insist that you did. Five minutes into his session you'll be forced to admit that maybe you didn't.

After our condensed draft preparation the year before, having so long to work out in Wellington was awesome, and we spent the time trying out new exercises in the gym and new moves on the court. I kept working on my shooting with Kenny, who had me shooting everything—layups, mid-range, and even three-pointers. I got to spend some time in Rotorua with the family and to go out on the farm again, although this time I was more understanding of the injury risks that come with farming.

I was also more aware of the risks that now came with doing anything at all. I'd been recognizable before the NBA just because of my size and the occasional news piece, but after making the conference finals (which even the part-time NBA fans watch) and actually getting good court time, I was suddenly a legit star, as gross as that sounds. I wasn't necessarily at the level of being "famous in New Zealand," but I was famous to any hard-out basketball fans *and* I was from New Zealand. So in that first off-season there were a ridiculous number of media requests and people stopping me on the street. It seemed everyone wanted to get a bit of time with Steven Adams.

To be honest, I kind of hated it and still do. The kids are great. If a kid comes up to me and wants an autograph or a photo, I'm all good so long as they have manners. But when it's an adult, I can't help thinking: *Why do you care?* Most adults who talk to me in public start off as if we've known each other for years and it makes me think maybe we have. But then they ask for a photo and suddenly it's weird. Why does a grown man, who probably has a good job and a nice family, want a photo with me just because I play basketball? To me, it's the same as me asking my doctor for a photo. I suppose it's the selfie world we're living in, and I appreciate my fans, but it gets old after a while.

I guess I don't get it because I was never starstruck by anyone (except Pop, and I'd never speak to him unless he spoke to me first because he's Pop). For me, the only reason to get starstruck is if you see someone who's doing what you want to do. And if you ever meet someone who's at a place where you want to be eventually, don't waste the opportunity by asking for a photo. Ask them for advice instead.

Because of this mindset, I'm always more than happy to answer basketball or school questions from kids of any age, and I'll gladly sign autographs for kids as I can see how something like that might motivate them somehow. But people my age or older asking for a photo? Come on, mate, you know we've both got better things we could be doing with our time.

By the end of the off-season I was kind of glad to be getting back to the solitude and routine of a new season in OKC.

Scotty Brooks had me and Dre starting in the preseason games, both to give the experienced players more rest and to see how we would work as part of the first unit. In every team there's the first unit (the starters) and the second unit (the bench with maybe one starter). I'd spent my rookie season as part of the second unit, so if I was going to start in the new season I'd have to get used to working with a different unit. Perk was still there and beating me up in practice, but I think we both knew that I might be starting as early as the first games of the regular season. I'm sure it bothered Perk, who was a veteran of the game, but he didn't let it affect how we practiced and he just kept going at me the same, which helped both of us.

Preseason was much the same as the year before. This time I was a tad more comfortable because I didn't think I was at risk of being relegated to the development league, but there was a different kind of pressure now. I knew I was being considered for the starting center position so I still needed to impress. The one play I still remember vividly is the first three-point attempt I ever took in the NBA. We were playing the Clippers (the bloody Clippers I tell ya) and I hadn't shot a three in a game in maybe three years. I definitely hadn't planned to shoot anywhere beyond the arc, but the shot clock was running down and we were scrambling for a loose ball. Suddenly, I had the ball at the top of the key with one second left to shoot. I turned in a panic, let it fly, and got a massive air ball. It was an air ball because it was too weak, but also an air ball because it wasn't straight. I somehow shot a double air ball. I haven't shot a three in a game since then.

When Scotty named the starting five for our first regular

season game against the Portland Trail Blazers a week later, Dre and I were both on it. It was cool to be draft buddies from the year before and both starting on a conference finals team. But it was also bittersweet because KD was injured. He had fractured his foot halfway through preseason and ended up missing the first 17 games of the season. Russ took up the number-one spot, but only for a few games, and then he was out for 14 games with a hand injury.

As everyone knew, without Russ and KD, we had our work cut out for us. Reggie Jackson stepped into the starting point guard spot for 14 games and led the scoring for most of them, but we still lost 10 of those 14 games, at one point losing six on the trot. After 16 games in the regular season we were 4–12 and very much out of playoff contention. When KD and Russ finally came back, we went on a winning streak and soon were looking like we might just scrape into the eighth position.

It's a point of pride for me that I never miss a game or a training unless I absolutely have to, and even then it's usually because a coach or trainer insists I rest. If there's literally anything I can do to play, I will. But what I can't do is control my migraines. I started getting them when I was 14, shortly after my dad died. Those two things are probably connected, but we haven't been able to figure it out completely yet. Half an hour before we were to play the Cavs at home in January, I sat in the locker room and watched as the vision in my left eye got narrower and narrower.

I knew straight away that I was done for the night. Once the vision starts to go, the excruciating headache comes in, followed by drowsiness and just generally feeling like shit. I swore to myself. I hadn't missed a single game since I was drafted and "I have a headache" sounded like such a weak excuse. But I could barely see or think, let alone get up and play against LeBron James.

I called out to one of the medics and told him that I'd be out for the game. As soon as he saw my discomfort, he rushed off to tell the coaching staff. I'm stubborn as hell and never want to show anyone that I'm hurting, so for me to ask for something to ease the pain was big. But even as they gave me some quite strong meds and the pain went away, I knew I would be hopeless out on the court. I sat in the locker room all game, pissed off that I had let my team down. We lost that game as well, which only made it worse. I vowed not to miss another game all season because our team had had enough injury setbacks as it was.

I managed to keep that vow for six games. Then I broke my hand playing against the Clippers. I swear to God that when I look back on the all noteworthy moments, both good and bad, in my career, the Clippers are somehow always there. Maybe some of their famous curse rubbed off on me and caused my injury.

I went up for a rebound and was hacked on my right hand. I knew straight away that something was broken because I couldn't make a fist. I still had two free throws to shoot, so I shot them left-handed. I actually made one of them, which means my left-handed free throw shooting is just as good as my right-handed. We deliberately fouled immediately and I sprinted straight to the changing rooms, before I could accidentally knock it again and make it worse. I was like Forrest Gump when he scores that touchdown and just keeps running right out of the stadium.

After an MRI, it was confirmed that I had a fractured metacarpal, which would require surgery to put a metal rod in next to the bone. I had the surgery the next morning—they don't muck around—and was told I would be out for at least three weeks. At any other point in the season, three weeks could mean up to 14 games. Russ's injury was very similar, and he missed 14 games. But because it was right before the All-Star break I was out for a full month, yet only missed 11 games. Eleven games is a lot to miss, but after KD's and Russ's injuries that same season, 11 games didn't seem so bad.

As a team, we just couldn't catch a break. Besides the break in my hand. And Russ's hand. And KD's foot. So really we caught a lot of breaks.

For a professional athlete, there honestly is nothing worse than being injured. *Getting* injured is always painful, but *being* injured can suck the life out of you from the inside. While most people think that coming back from injury takes a lot of physical work—which is true—it's keeping your mental game up when you are unable to play that requires all the energy. My injury period of one month was short compared to those guys who tear ACLs in their knee or just straight up break a leg. Even so, I was going a bit crazy by the time I got to play again.

As it was my hand that was injured, the coaches made sure I worked the rest of my body twice as hard. And because shooting, passing, and scrimmaging (all the fun parts of training) involve hands, I spent most of my time on the treadmill or on the bike or on some other machine that is designed to ruin your day. Like the off-season, not being able to play in games when you're injured means you are at risk of letting your fitness levels drop dangerously. I foolishly thought that being injured would suck because it would be boring to not play, but worse than that, it sucked because it was physically so much harder than playing.

Up until my injury I had been playing well. I wasn't suddenly putting up huge numbers, but they had always been improving. Part of that would be because of the extra playing time I was getting, but I also felt myself getting more and more comfortable in the first unit and knowing what plays worked well and opened up opportunities for me to score.

When I got injured in early February, Perk subbed in for me. When I came back to play again in early March, Perk was gone. He had been traded to the Utah Jazz. I was gutted to see him go, but it looked like it could be a good move for him. The trade itself involved three teams and way too many players to keep track of, but we ended up getting Enes Kanter, who I knew was good because I never enjoyed playing against him. We also lost Reggie Jackson in that trade but, to be honest, I wasn't that sad to see him go and I'm pretty confident the feeling was mutual.

The Thunder organization works because every single person knows exactly what their role is and performs it well. I, for one, was thriving in my role as the new starting center thanks to the continued guidance from Perk and Nick. However, Reggie didn't like his role. When KD and Russ were both injured, Reggie became the starting point guard and therefore a team leader. We all knew he thought he could go up against the best point guards in the league because he was the only one who ever complained about court time. Ever.

During those 14 games Russ was out, he got his wish. Although he scored well and his stats looked good, we weren't clicking on the floor. I knew it, Perk knew it, Scotty knew it, probably every-one knew just from looking at our win–loss record. Reggie didn't really know it.

When Russ came back from injury and took over the starting spot again, Reggie wasn't happy. We were just looking at him thinking, "You've got to be some kind of fool to seriously think you should be starting over Russ." But that's exactly what he thought, and that kind of thinking went against everything the Thunder was about. Yes, we competed in practices and fought for the starting positions, but once the actual game starts we all do whatever is required of us, no matter how much or how little.

When the trade deadline got near, we knew Reggie wanted to leave. And because we knew he wanted to leave, we wanted him to leave as well. Why would we want to work every day with someone who wanted to be somewhere else? When he was finally traded to the Detroit Pistons we forgot about him pretty quickly because we had new guys to welcome to the team. The guy who I immediately connected with was Enes because we were both bigs and had the same hustle. It was a little weird to have a guy my age join the bigs practice after spending my rookie season going up against old guys like Perk and Nick. We were almost the same height and a similar weight, we were both overseas recruits and we both talked a lot of shit in practice. The only difference was he talked shit with a Turkish accent. In other words, we were a bromance waiting to happen.

Enes was just as vocal as Reggie during games but was the complete opposite. Sometimes when guys get traded it can take them time to get used to the new team, and you can see some of their old team habits hanging around. Not Enes. As soon as he walked into our locker room, he was a Thunder guy. His fierce loyalty went wherever he went, so as soon as he arrived in Oklahoma he was ready to put his body on the line for his team-mates. We respected that and encouraged it. He might have talked more in one game than I'd spoken in a whole season, but it didn't matter. Different personalities can work well on a team as long as everyone has the same goal.

Enes arrived in the middle of my injury month and had his work cut out for him, with me injured and Perk traded. He didn't hesitate for a second and did the work of two big men. It was surreal seeing someone wearing the Thunder uniform and playing my position, executing in all the areas I had been trying to improve. But, at the same time, he was new to the team and didn't know all the plays, which is where I came in.

Getting traded mid-season meant there was literally one day of transition before Enes threw on a singlet and played for us, so he had to learn on the fly. I don't think anyone would have predicted me helping out trade recruits in my second season, but I loved the extra responsibility. Every time he came out of the game and onto the bench, I made sure he sat next to me so I could explain what plays we were running and what we were doing on defense. When he picked it up quickly, I let him know he was doing good. He seemed surprised by that. I guess he was used to competing for the spot, not working together to make the team succeed.

When I was finally cleared to play against the Toronto Raptors exactly one month after the fracture, I started on the bench. Being cleared to play doesn't mean you are 100 percent healthy.

My hand could work just fine, but it was stiff from underuse and still caused a lot of pain when I caught the ball a certain way.

It took a long time before I could get through a full game without needing a massage or ice to help with the pain. I started to think of all the games I had played without pain and how I had taken them for granted. It was a bit like when you get a toothache and immediately start remembering how you never thanked your teeth for not hurting before.

In the week before my injury we had played the New Orleans Pelicans in back-to-back games. It doesn't happen often in a season, and it almost feels like a mini playoff series. We won the first game on their turf despite KD being out injured again (he was injured a lot that season). Then two nights later we were back in OKC and playing them again. It was a tied game, 113–113, with one second to go, and the Pelicans had the inbound. They gave it to their star Anthony Davis, and he sank a buzzer-beater three for the win.

We were gutted. Every win counts and every win when you've got injured players feels a bit sweeter. But we didn't dwell on it because it was one game in an 82-game season and probably wouldn't make a whole lot of difference by the time the playoffs came around. Little did we know that one particular loss would come back to bite us in the arse.

As we settled in with our new teammates and headed into the final stretch of games, we got used to playing without KD. His foot had given him more problems when I was also injured, and he sat out for a few weeks. We thought he might make it back for the last bunch of games, but he got surgery at the end of March and was out for the rest of the season.

We had a good run of wins in March, but for our last 10 games we came up against most of the top-placed teams and went on a losing streak. By the time our last game of the regular season finally rolled around, most of us just wanted the season to be finished. I'd missed 12 games, Russ had missed 15, and KD had missed 55.

We were tied with the Pelicans on 44 wins and 37 losses, and we were placed at eighth and ninth in the standings. The outcomes of our final regular-season match-ups would determine who went to the playoffs and who didn't. We had the advantage playing the last-placed Timberwolves, while the Pelicans were up against the Spurs.

We went out and beat the Timberwolves in time to catch the moment the Pelicans beat the Spurs. Because we were tied on the table, the team to advance would be the one that won the most games in our regular season series against each other. The Pelicans won our season head-to-head 3–1. Anthony Davis's buzzer-beater to win game four had sent the Pelicans to the playoffs and the Thunder somewhere they hadn't been since 2009—the post-season bottom seven.

In a way it was good we didn't make the playoffs. KD would still have been injured and there is no way we would have gone far without him, especially with Russ and me still working through issues with our hands. A long off-season would be good for everyone to rest their bodies and recover after a sluggish, painful six months of basketball.

We went away relieved to have a break and I left Oklahoma immediately. I left so quickly that I found out via Twitter that Scott Brooks had been fired as our head coach. Of course it came as a shock to me. We had clearly had a crappy season, but the reasons for it were easy to see. All you had to do was look at the regular line-up of players wearing suits instead of uniforms at our games.

I left at the end of the season expecting to come back to Scotty's coaching at the beginning of the next season. Perhaps it was my naivety, but I had absolutely no idea that there was even a chance he would be fired because of our performance that season. He was the OKC Thunder coach and had been with Russ and KD from the start. He was tight with everyone, which is what made it even stranger to find out online that he had been fired. Since then I've seen that is how it works for almost every player and coach. We all find out what's happening to our teammates, and sometimes ourselves, by checking the Twitter page of ESPN's Adrian Wojnarowski.

It took less than two weeks for Thunder management to hire a new head coach—and once again I found out who he was via Twitter. Billy Donovan was the hugely successful coach of the University of Florida, which with him as coach had been one of the most successful college basketball teams in the past two decades. I read articles about Scotty's firing to see what the reasons for it were because it definitely wasn't the players complaining. I felt kinda stink about it while I was in New Zealand on break, but I soon told myself I had better get used to it because the NBA is a business, and a cutthroat one at that.

I spent my first two weeks in New Zealand relaxing for the first time in years. My school mates and I went wine tasting. As far as money went, food and wine were about the only things I spent it on. I still hadn't bought a house, and rent in Oklahoma City is comparatively cheap. I hadn't bought a car because a dealer loaned me a nice Ford pickup truck. I never wore jewelery so I wasn't going out dropping thousands of dollars on chain necklaces or earrings. When you have simple needs, it's almost hard to spend your money.

What I did happily indulge in was wine. You probably wouldn't think it, but I know my way around a fine merlot. Apparently, Pop also loves a drop, and I'm still developing an elaborate plan that will see us going on a wine tour of Italy together. It involves an inbound pass from the Spurs bench, a succinct and flawless one-liner from me before I pass the ball in, and then playing it cool, leaving it to Pop to make the next move. This is the sort of stuff I start thinking about when I have too much time on my hands.

While I was home, the Adams clan had a mini reunion in Rotorua. It was our first one since 2005, but not much had changed for the kids. I'd gone from being the shortest to the tallest in the family photo, but otherwise I was still the baby. Sid, Ralph, and Warren were the only absentees. We tried to re-create the photo from 2005, but it wasn't the same. Everyone had gotten a bit wider and we weren't in Dad's big backyard like before. And, of course, the old man wasn't standing in the middle as the anchor.

I got another tattoo added to my arm, but realized I couldn't keep doing that every year or I'd soon have no more body left. Instead I decided to wait for big moments before adding anything. Big moments like an NBA Championship.

I told Kenny and Gav I wanted to travel. I had never been anywhere just for fun, and it seemed like something I should do while I could afford it. I could tell they were a bit hesitant because I'd never been let loose on the world without a basketball coach or trainer nearby to make sure I was keeping up with my workouts. But they needn't have worried. I was going to see my sister Val in Switzerland.

Val had been based there for a couple years with her new coach Jean-Pierre Egger. I thought that my life as a professional athlete was physically tough, but after spending a few days training with Val I realized I had it so good.

At the time, Val was by some stretch the world's best woman shot-putter—a two-time Olympic champion, four-time world champion, and IAAF Women's Athlete of the Year. She hadn't lost a meet in five years. She was about as dominant as an athlete could possibly be at world level, yet she lived very differently from her younger brother who played basketball seven months a year and would have been glad to be considered in the top 500 players in the world. Part of the issue was that athletics generally isn't as lucrative a sport as basketball. But a lot of it was simply because she's a woman.

Val was living and training in Magglingen, a small Swiss town with a world-class athletic training facility owned by the government. The people who trained there were all full-time, world-class athletes. None of them were rich, though, including Val. She had based herself there because that's where the best facilities and coaching were. And she was willing to live anywhere if it helped her performance. But she was alone over there and had to be her own motivator when things got tough. She lived in a single room with a shower and toilet. It was small for a regular-sized person and tiny for an Adams.

Val took me to one of her trainings and I nearly died. Lots of guys look at (most) NBA players and see strong men at the peak of their physical fitness. Those same guys probably look at strong women and think they could still beat them in an arm wrestle. I've never been foolish enough to think that because, with a sister like Val, I know better.

I was keen to train with her because I hadn't seen her properly in a few years and we both seemed to be in the best shape of our lives. With that classic Adams competitiveness, things got interesting in the gym. Except I couldn't even do the work she was doing, let alone do it well. My gym routines had involved a lot of core stability work, building up some leg muscle (but not too much), and occasionally some heavy deadlifting.

Val was throwing around weights that I didn't even want to stand next to in case I got injured.

I told her I couldn't risk getting injured trying new lifts so she took me through her other workouts for speed, explosiveness, and agility. If you think shot-putters just need to be strong, think again. Her vertical was almost better than mine and she would kill the standard basketball agility tests. It was amazing finally getting to see my sister in her element, and I wasn't at all surprised to see her huge work ethic given she was an Adams kid.

Even though there's a nine-year age gap between us and we didn't grow up together, Val and I have a lot in common and are arguably the most similar of all my siblings. A bunch of us could have been world-class athletes if the circumstances had been right and the commitment had been there, but Val and I were the only two with enough of a single-track mind to stick at it long term.

I will always have massive respect for Val and everything she's accomplished. Being a woman in sport means doing the same amount of work as men for a fraction of the reward, so only those who are truly passionate and driven stick around at the top for as long as she has. There were no multimillion-dollar contracts or hugely lucrative sponsorships, there was just enough money for her to train and get by from tournament to tournament.

Growing up and watching Val as she moved up in the world of athletics, I knew that it was even more possible to be a professional athlete if you had the Adams genes and work ethic. Getting to the NBA wasn't a pipe dream for me, it was a realistic possibility thanks to my genes and the drive I had inherited from my dad and my older siblings.

I spent two weeks with Val in Switzerland, trained well, and attempted to throw the shot put for the first time since high school. I was way stronger than I was in school and it probably went further than my PB, but Val laughed at me anyway.

A month later Val had to return to Auckland for surgery and I made sure I was there when it happened. Undergoing surgery when a healthy body is what keeps you employed makes it a much bigger deal than when you work in an office. I had had a similar experience with my hand, and it was good to talk about the struggles of going through rehab and trying to get back to peak fitness.

It was a good, long off-season and by the time I got back to OKC for training camp I was well and truly ready for a better Thunder

OKC TEAM ROSTER 2015–16

STEVEN ADAMS, center

D. J. AUGUSTIN, guard

NICK COLLISON, forward

KEVIN "KD" DURANT, forward

RANDY FOYE, guard

JOSH HUESTIS, forward

SERGE IBAKA, forward

ENES KANTER, center

MITCH MCGARY, forward

NAZR MOHAMMED, center

ANTHONY MORROW, guard

STEVE NOVAK, forward

CAMERON PAYNE, guard

ANDRE "DRE" ROBERSON, guard

KYLE SINGLER, forward

DION WAITERS, guard

RUSSELL "RUSS" WESTBROOK, guard

season. Everyone came back to training with a chip on their shoulder. The last season was in the past and we were ready to take full advantage of the team we had, now that we were all healthy again. Much like players come and go quite seamlessly, Billy Donovan settled in quickly as the new head coach. There weren't many other changes because we had pretty much the same roster.

We started our preseason how we planned to continue, with everyone playing in a win over the Spurs. We hadn't played a game with a full-strength squad in what seemed like forever, and it reminded us just how good we were as a unit. KD was back, though not pushing too hard in the preseason. Russ was back—and he doesn't know how to not push hard. Enes was now a core part of the team and Dre was becoming our key defensive guy. As for me, I had some new moves I'd been working on that were finally ready to start seeing court time.

Every player works on new moves all the time. Some players will work on something for a week and then try it out in a game. Others work for a month before going public with it. I work on a move for seasons before any fan sees it. It's not that it wouldn't work or that it takes me ages to learn it, I just like to go for the sure option, and a brand-new move is hardly ever the sure option.

When I first arrived in OKC, the things I knew I could do for sure were rebound and dunk. Everyone else had all other areas covered, so I just did those two things and worked hard on my defense. But in the gym, MB put me straight to work learning the floater. I'd done floaters before with Kenny, but MB made floaters *the* shot. Every single practice I shot floaters—every kind of floater. No dribble, one dribble, from the elbow, off a spin . . . every sort. No matter what else we did during our bigs practice, shooting floaters was in there.

MB wanted to make it so that shooting a floater would be as instinctive as going up for an easy dunk. I wasn't bad at them, even in the beginning, but it took a long while before I started to bring them out regularly in games. Even though it was an option for me, I figured any shot that Russ or KD took was probably a better option than me taking a mid-range floater. And I was right.

Floaters and hook shots are MB's two non-negotiables. With the way the NBA is getting faster and big guys are playing as guards, every post player has to have a hook shot. Ask MB and he'll talk for hours about why a hook shot is as important to a center as a layup, maybe even more important. I feel like I've shot more hook shots and more floaters in my life than I've thought thoughts.

We get 15 minutes with MB before we practice as a full team. Sometimes that will be 15 minutes of nothing but floaters. Sometimes it will be 15 minutes of only jump hooks. Sometimes it will be all post moves: drop step, or rip to the middle. Or it will be a seal day; I'll seal a guy and he'll throw it up to me. If you miss, you go again until you make it. But hooks will always be there, and floaters will always be there. They weren't foreign shots to me, but I had never practiced them so much before moving to OKC.

One particular move that MB wanted me to work on was the quick spin on the baseline. It's a good move. When you get the ball low in the post, the natural instinct is to pivot back into the middle where there is more space. With the baseline right there, it's also natural to defend heavily on the open side to force a player to go baseline and risk dribbling out-of-bounds or trapping themselves. The baseline spin that MB showed me was a tight, quick, full pivot towards the baseline, using the defender's body as an anchor. It's meant to be done without needing to dribble at all. But because there's no dribble, the footwork has to be impeccable or you'll be called for a travel.

MB showed me that move early in my rookie season and we practiced it regularly all season before I was able to try it out in a game. The thing with me is that I only like to take high-percentage shots. Even as a rookie, I had one of the highest field goal percentages in the team because I made sure that the few shots I took were almost always going to go in. When you have stars on your team, it would be foolish to take risky shots because there are so many other options. With that mindset, a new move has to be damn near perfect before I use it in a game.

By the start of the 2015–16 season, I had managed to extend my high-percentage range to include mid-range hooks and floaters. But what I knew would be most helpful to our stacked team was to be a force on defense and on the boards. Every game and every practice I worked on my off-ball work—countering a box-out, predicting shots, and shutting down open space. It was all stuff that wasn't exactly new but took a lot of court time to fully learn. I also felt I was finally comfortable reading other teams' systems and knowing their strengths and weaknesses.

We started off a bit slow, ending up on 11–7 by the end of November. We weren't worried, though. We had a new coach and a fresh, fitter team compared to the last season, so we were just warming up.

By the end of the year we were 23–10. We were gaining momentum and I was developing a pretty sweet pick-and-roll chemistry with Russ. He had told me right from the beginning, "If I'm driving to the hoop, I'm looking for you, so be ready." While he meant it in 2013, I wasn't always ready. But after two years of toughening up my screens and working on my above-the-rim work, our pick-and-rolls were looking good.

Alley-oop dunks aren't necessarily harder than any other shot in the game, they're just not as common, which means you've got to practice them. Leaving the ground, catching the ball, finding the hoop, and dunking it before you land is a lot of stuff to think about. If you've ever played that game where you try to catch a pass as you are jumping into a swimming pool, you'll know how easy it is to get wrong. But after a couple of hundred games spent on the same court with the same hoops, knowing where you are in relation to the basket becomes a sixth sense.

As soon as I got my first alley-oop off Russ's pass I realized that it was in fact a high-percentage look. His passing is pinpoint and almost impossible to defend against so all I had to do was make sure I got up to guide the ball to the basket. Easy as.

It's funny how it's those pick-and-roll alley-oops that always end up on the highlight reels when most of the time it's the contested rebounds and putbacks that are the toughest shots to execute. Too bad they never get put on a poster.

The most important difference for us at the end of the

season was that the workload was being distributed evenly, or at least more so than in past seasons. In one of our last games, we came up against Enes's old team, the Jazz. I could tell he was nervous because he couldn't seem to do anything the whole first half he was so hyped up. As we came out for the second half I pulled him aside and told him, mustached man to mustached man, to just breathe. Now I'm not trying to say that I'm the Enes whisperer, but he went out and dropped 16 in the second half. Six of us scored in double figures that game, a stark contrast to the 2014 playoffs when six Spurs did that and only three of our guys. Even though we were ranked third in the Western Conference, it felt like 2016 would be the year we became NBA Champions.

There was no point trying to finish at the top of the Western Conference table. That spot belonged to the Warriors before the season was even half over. They were the defending champions and had started the season with a 24–0 run. They finished the regular season 73–9, a new NBA record for the most regular-season wins. We played them three times in the regular season and lost to them three times.

At the end of March, we were well positioned in the top four and had little risk of finishing below that by the end of the season. We ended the season a bit shaky, but when you know you are into the playoffs safely, and there's no chance of moving up or down the ladder, it's easy to take your foot off the pedal and start looking ahead to the first playoff series.

I thought I had won the game for us. Imagine that, a buzzer-beater to win a game in the playoffs. It was game two of the series against my old mate Dirk Nowitzki and the Mavericks, and I got a tip-in basket right on the buzzer to put us up by one. Or so I thought.

Even though we were the higher seed, a lot of pundits had picked us to bow out in the first round because of our below-average end run in the regular season. We never paid attention to them to begin with, but it was interesting to see that people thought so little of our potential to win the whole thing. We planned to get in, win it in four, then get out. Why wouldn't we?

It started well at home with a 37-point win. It was my first playoff start and a good one for me to get used to playing at that intensity for twice as many minutes as the previous play-off series I was in. None of us had a spectacular game; we just all played well together, which was even better. I'd noticed that while all my stats were going up—minutes, points, rebounds— my block numbers were going down. And that's because I was learning how to make the stops *before* a block was required. Nick had been working with me a lot that season, helping me read movements on the court and shut down a shot before it's even in motion. The block tally was actually a stat I was happy to see go down.

After the whipping we dished out in game one, we should have done exactly the same thing in game two. But, as all good NBA teams do, the Mavericks figured out what we liked and adjusted to counter it—meaning they slowed the game right down. They managed to bring the pace of the game practically down to a walk and it threw us out of whack. We looked okay on transition, because that was our strength, but everything was practically the opposite of game one.

Nobody seemed to be able to do anything on our team. Our shooting was trash while the Mavs' point guard Raymond Felton embarrassed us by getting 21 points and 14 rebounds. It's a Loss with a capital L when a 6'1" point guard drives to the basket and scores a layup over your 7-foot self. After scoring 108 in game one, trailing 85–84 with seven seconds to go seemed ridiculous. But after shooting two from 15 field goals in the final five minutes, we should have been losing by a lot more.

Felton was shooting two free throws with 7.1 seconds on the clock and a one-point lead. If he made both, we needed to set up KD or Russ for a three to tie the game. If he made one, well, we had some options. And if he missed both, we just had to transition like we knew how and go for a layup to win. He missed both.

KD got the rebound and headed down the court before passing ahead to Russ. I turned and sprinted, but they were the two quickest guys on the court and had the two lanes covered so I made sure to at least block Felton's way at the top of the key. Russ drove down the middle towards three defenders and dished to KD who went up for the layup. It was tipped by someone and missed. Russ tapped it back and that also missed. I grabbed the ball as it fell and, as quick as I could, tipped it back into the hoop as the buzzer went. The ball dropped through the net and I thought I had won the game for us.

The whole stadium thought we had won. The bench swarmed the court and mobbed me. The score read OKC 86–DAL 85. But when the refs reviewed the play and the slow-mo went up on the jumbotron, it was hard to argue. The ball definitely looked like it was still touching my hand when the clock ran out. I'd say there was less than 0.1 second in it. But 0.1 second doesn't matter when there were a hundred different things that could have won the game for us if we had executed correctly. That's the thing with playoff basketball, you can't afford to let your focus drift for even a second because every play could be the play that wins or loses the game for you. And every game could be the game that wins or loses a series.

As soon as the call was overturned and the scoreboard returned to displaying a Mavs win, I thanked the refs and headed straight for the locker room. We had work to do. We weren't going to win a championship playing like that.

Our wake-up call at our home arena worked. We went to Dallas with something to prove, and we proved it by rolling them at home, 131–102.

In game four we made sure not to get complacent again and won by 11, never once giving up the lead throughout the whole game. Heading home for game five we knew we had to end the series there to give us a decent rest before the second round.

There is a huge difference between playing five games with five days' rest between series and playing seven games with two days' rest. The memory of our last game at home was still fresh and we had to erase it with a big win. So we did. We won by 16 in a fairly one-sided match. I played my best game of the series with 15 points and 10 rebounds, and I hoped to keep building from there and into the next series against our dreaded friendly foes, the Spurs.

Whatever momentum we thought we had going into the series was quickly stopped by the second-seeded Spurs. They were heavy favorites after finishing the regular season with

67 wins. If the Warriors hadn't broken seemingly every NBA record under the sun that year, everyone would have been talking about what a crazy regular season the Spurs had. The Cavaliers, who dominated the Eastern Conference, had only 55 wins, the same as us who were third place in the West. The Spurs' squad still had all the veterans but had added LaMarcus Aldridge. In four playoff meetings, the Thunder had never won a series against the Spurs.

After one game we hadn't convinced anyone that we were about to break tradition. Playing in San Antonio, it took only one quarter for them to remind us why they were one of the greats. They outscored us 43–20 in the first quarter, something that had never happened to us before. And it didn't get any better.

Aldridge and Kawhi Leonard were on fire, and when those two were on fire at the same time they were near unstoppable. We lost by 32 points, at one stage trailing by 43. It was embarrassing but, again, it was one game. And it was the first game at that. We still had a long way to go in the series and plenty of time to regroup.

In game two we did exactly what Dallas had done to us in game two a fortnight earlier. We came back when nobody expected it, contested one of the most exciting games of the play-offs, and won by one in front of their home crowd. And just like our game two against Dallas, the final moments were a shambles that led to a lot of complaining on both sides of the court. I wasn't complaining. We won and I had a good double-double with 12 points and 17 rebounds.

We gave the Spurs plenty of chances to win, particularly when we stuffed up an inbound pass with 13 seconds to go. I ended up defending a three-on-one situation, and that's when your balls are tested. Deciding which way to go—whether to hedge or drop back—needs to be done in a split second. I made the right decision (well, we won so it can't have been that wrong) and the Spurs were allowed only one final shot.

Patty Mills took it—a corner three—and I sprinted out to him and lunged at his shot, tipping it so it fell short. My momentum carried me into the front row, but I'd had no time to check my surroundings. There were still two seconds on the clock.

When I turned around to rush back into play, a hand was on my forearm, holding me back. I yanked my arm away from the fan as the buzzer went. When I turned to see who it was that was about to get a hiding, I saw it was a woman. Call me sexist, but I assumed she must have been trying to keep her balance and grabbed whatever was in front of her, which was my arm. This might not be true; she might have been deliberately keeping me out of the play to help her team. But at that point we had won, so I stopped caring what her motives were.

Game three, our first at home, went to the Spurs after a lackluster effort from us. I played 41 minutes but put up only one shot. The ball just wasn't moving a lot and we weren't executing our plays how they were intended: 2–1 to the Spurs.

We had a chance to redeem ourselves at home on Mother's Day and we took it. I had learned a lot in the two years since I'd last matched up with Tim Duncan in the playoffs. At the very least, I wasn't going to fall for his kind of trash talk again. Instead, something incredible happened. He started the game but only played 12 minutes—and in those 12 minutes he didn't shoot at all. I found out after the game that was the first time in his entire career that he hadn't taken a single shot. He might have been tired, he might have been sick, but I had been working hard on my defense and it felt good to be able to shut down someone like Duncan, even for 12 minutes. After a terrible first quarter, we fought back to win 111–97, and I equaled my playoffs career high of 16 points. It was a good game.

Heading back to San Antonio, we were well aware that they had lost only one game at home the whole regular season. But our last game in their home stadium was a win to us, so we felt like we held the advantage. We led for the first half and then kind of crumbled and gave them the lead for most of the second half. But it doesn't matter who leads for the whole game, what's important is who is leading when that final buzzer sounds. We won 95–91 to take the lead in the series and have a chance at finishing it at home.

In the last tip-off of Tim Duncan's NBA career, we both missed the ball. I didn't know it was his last game because I didn't know who was going to win, or even that he was planning to announce his retirement in the off-season.

I had had a migraine before the game, but no way was I going to sit out a playoff match. The medical team pumped me with fluids and pain meds and I made it out in time to warm up.

It should have been a blowout. We were up by 28 but let them go on a run in the fourth quarter and get back to within 10. Dre and I actually came through for our team and it was maybe the first game we showed fans that both of us were going to be Thunder staples in years to come.

After being somewhat quiet the whole series, Tim Duncan came to life in that last game and scored 19 points. I got 15, in what felt like the first and last time that I truly matched up with him. We scrapped the whole game, right down to the last few plays as we led by over 10 points. It was an honor and a privilege to be the great Tim Duncan's final opponent. What a legend.

We went into the series against the Spurs as heavy underdogs after they had one of the best regular seasons in recent history. For us to win in six was the perfect warm-up to play the team that had just had *the* best regular season in history. We were heading to the conference finals to play the formidable Warriors.

15.

SAY A PRAYER FOR MY TESTICLES

People say I have a face that's easy to punch. And balls that are easy to kick. It's hard to argue when you're sitting in the locker room with ice on your nuts.

The 2016 conference finals against the Warriors was when I became a household name in America. Unfortunately, the reason I became a household name wasn't my stellar play but because I got kicked in the nuts by Draymond Green. Twice. Let me explain.

The Warriors were the favorites, no matter how you looked at it. They were reigning champions, had just broken the record for most wins in a regular season, and they looked unstoppable. They were basically the Spurs if everyone on the Spurs was a perimeter shooter.

For almost every opponent in the NBA, you keep the same game plan. There might be tweaks depending on what systems they run, but it's pretty much the same.

The 2016 Warriors were the first team that required a complete overhaul in our approach. They didn't play a variation of the same game like everyone else, they played something new and faster, with more ball movement and a stupidly high field-goal percentage. They played small ball, the smallest ball in the league. We were the aggressors, the big, hulking, number-one rebounding team in the regular season.

Even before it began, people knew it would be a series to remember.

Game one at Golden State

It started out shit. We couldn't seem to make a shot and somehow neither could the Warriors. It took a good four minutes before either side could settle into a rhythm. Russ was getting beaten up. He went down hard on the first play of the game and then caught an elbow to the face from Andrew Bogut going up for a rebound. The Warriors might have been the small team in the match-up, but they had Bogut and Draymond Green, two guys known for their physical play.

I enjoyed going up against Bogut. We both liked to annoy our opponents and were able to take a lot of contact from each other without the refs getting involved. I took a knock to my nose early in the second quarter and it bled. Any blood means you are subbed off until it stops, but I wasn't ready to quit yet so we stuffed some cotton up my left nostril and back out I went. By then, a bleeding nostril was the least of my worries. My injured hand had flared up again.

It looked like nothing. Bogut had the ball at the top of the key and my right hand was on him as a block. When he swung around to pass, the movement in his arm tweaked my thumb and a pain worse than almost anything I had felt shot through my hand and up my arm. The original injury had happened 15 months earlier but was still causing me problems. For the rest of the game, my right hand was swollen and trembling uncontrollably. I did my best to ignore it.

Ignoring pain is quite easy once you get your mind into the game. Everything else—the crowd, the noise, any niggles you have—disappears. All you think about is the next play. It's in the pauses, the free throws, the play reviews, the time on the bench that the pain suddenly rushes back into focus.

We knew that first game would be crucial in slowing the Warriors' momentum. We had lost all three of our regular-season games against them, so we had to get a win now. I was doing what I could with my bung hand, but getting blocked by Draymond didn't help things. He threw it down to Klay Thompson for a fast break layup and Klay was blocked even harder by Serge. That's how you avenge your teammates.

KD shot a three to tie the game at the start of the fourth quarter. With four minutes to go we were in the lead, but we still had a lot of work to do. People loved to talk about how often we let leads go in the last five minutes during the regular-season. We hadn't done it in the playoffs yet, but it was a hard trend to ignore.

With a minute to go and a one-point lead, I scrambled for a loose ball, ended up at the top of the key and had a decision to make. I could hold it up, kick it back out for someone else to take the shot, or I could take it myself. My instinct in those situations had been to give the ball to someone else for a better shot, but in that moment I backed myself and drove. Draymond fouled me, and I was off to the free-throw line. The Warriors were probably happy about it because I had shot four from seven that game and only 60 percent from the line all season. I wasn't exactly a safe bet for two points. I breathed, ignored the pain in my hand, and swished both: 103–100.

Oracle Arena in Oakland, usually one of the loudest crowds in the country, was eerily quiet in that final minute as their team was forced to foul in search of a comeback. It didn't work. We had beaten the supposedly unstoppable Warriors on their home turf to draw first blood in the conference finals. It was a huge upset, but no one in our team was surprised.

Game two at Golden State

Nobody outside of Oklahoma seriously expected us to win game one. We didn't mind. In fact, we used it as fuel. There's nothing like a dismissive audience to get you fired up. But we knew the Warriors had shot uncharacteristically and wouldn't shoot that poorly all series. So we still had a lot of homework to do to try to figure how to shut down a squad full of shooting weapons.

Draymond hit a three at the start of the game and took the opportunity to get in my face about it. It didn't bother me. I know players trash talk to get a reaction, but that's something I don't do. I don't even bother trying to think of clever things to say to trash-talkers, so 99 percent of the time I say nothing. The first time I played against Kevin Garnett, arguably the most prolific trash-talker in the league, I was warned that he could talk a good game. He certainly could talk, but I'd heard variations of it all before. When I had had enough, I looked at him and said, "Sorry, no English." He stopped talking to me after that but must have been confused when I spoke English to all my teammates.

After my painful game two days earlier, I hoped to go as long as possible without the pain in my right hand flaring up again. But within five minutes it was back. I just had to get used to it. Moments later, I found myself reluctantly giving a Warrior a piggyback as he came down for a rebound. All his weight landed on my lower back and I folded in half before dropping to the floor. It felt like something in my back was out of place and I just had to get out of there. There is nothing worse than walking down the tunnel to the locker rooms when you can hear the game still being played behind you.

The medical team did some quick prods before I managed to get back on the court. It seemed to have been just a weird movement. I'd find out if it was something worse after the game.

The first kick to my nuts was actually the fourth time I ended up on the floor that game. Running back on transition defense, Draymond came down the length of the court and went up for a floater. As he went up, his knee went straight to my groin. It was a natural movement, but that didn't make it hurt any less. I went to the ground because that's the first instinct when you know you've been kicked in the groin. But it wasn't the worst kick I had received, and it certainly wasn't the most pain I had felt that game, so I didn't think much of it.

What was more painful was the fact that by the time we got going in the fourth quarter we were down 20 points. We were just being outplayed. The one consolation—if you could even call it that—was that we knew we weren't playing our best.

Coach Donovan started playing the bench with eight minutes still to go, that's how early we conceded. We didn't deserve to win that game and we tried to put it behind us as we flew home for game three.

Game three at Oklahoma City

The first kick was more to my shaft, but the second was straight in the balls. A direct hit right to my little fellas. If my stomach hadn't been shriveling up inside me, I might have been more impressed with the accuracy.

We were loving being back home in front of our fans and ready to give them a big win. It started well, for me at least. My hand was feeling steadier and I wasn't about to waste the pain-free minutes. I found myself guarding Steph Curry on the perimeter, which meant I was very far away from where I was supposed to be. I'm pretty quick on defense, but point guards are point guards for a reason and they should all be able to beat a center off the dribble. I saw Curry set up for a shot and jumped. If it turned out to be a fake, I could live with it. But I couldn't live with him shooting yet another three in my face. It wasn't a fake and I got a rare perimeter block on the reigning MVP. That play was a huge boost to keep hustling for touches on defense and not let anything get by.

Down the other end I got a putback basket and was well in the game. Soon I got to use the quick spin I had been working on with MB. I'd usually like to be firmly set before whipping it out, but playoff basketball forces everyone to step up. I drove to the hoop, spun, and drew the foul. All good stuff.

It wasn't just me who was playing with an extra level of

intensity, everyone was on form and we led throughout the whole game, running transition like only we knew how. The Warriors fought back to a tied game more than once, but we always managed to push the lead back out with more fast break points. Then halfway through the second quarter the kick happened.

Draymond caught the ball at the top of the key and tried to drive past me to the basket. I cut him off, managed to knock the ball out of his hands and next thing I knew I felt a shoe connect with my nutsack. It didn't hurt in the moment it happened, but I sank to my knees in preparation for the onslaught. I was running on adrenaline, which helped a lot, but Draymond's got power in his legs, I'll give him that.

Sure enough, a moment later the pain moved straight to my stomach, making me want to throw up. I didn't see the replay when it first showed on the big screen because I was hunched over trying to breathe and to not cry. But I heard the crowd's reaction. I had never heard booing quite like it. While I was working on not moving too much or standing up, I could hear a chant starting. It took me a few moments to figure out that 18,000 rarked-up fans were yelling "Kick him out! Kick him out!" The refs reviewed the play for quite a while, which gave me enough time to put my insides back together and check that I was still a man.

Eventually, they ruled it a Flagrant 1 technical foul, which meant I had to shoot free throws with my midsection feeling like it was trying to swallow itself. Somehow, I made both and went straight to the bench. I ended up with three fouls before the half and sat out for a long stretch of the game. It worked, though, because the Warriors had underestimated Dre's offensive assets and he came out on form that night. So did Dion Waiters.

In the final stretches of the half, I watched our team completely dominate the defending champions and it was beautiful. All second half we were swinging at the knees, enjoying the atmosphere and actually having fun. I almost forgot my balls were still hurting. After taking a hiding in Oakland, we took back the advantage, winning game three just as convincingly, 133–105.

People loved talking about me getting kicked in the nuts twice. The reporters asked about it after the game. There wasn't much to say. We won and that's all that mattered. Draymond said it was accidental and I had no reason to believe any non-psychopath would deliberately kick another man there. The play was reviewed again the following day and the call was upgraded to a Flagrant 2. Had it been called on the floor, Draymond would have been automatically ejected. Instead he copped a $25,000 fine and was cleared to play in game four.

A lot of fans thought he should have been suspended. I wanted him to be suspended simply because it meant I wouldn't have to go against him for a game. Only an idiot would say they didn't want Draymond Green on their team. Being able to defend every position is something not many players can do, and he's one of them. That made him a nuisance for us while trying to run our systems, so of course I wanted to see him sit out a game. But otherwise I didn't care. He kicked me, it hurt, so what? It's just basketball. There were, and are, more important things to worry about than figuring out what really happened.

In saying that, if he'd done the same thing to one of my teammates, I might have had a completely different reaction. I can handle people taking cheap shots at me all day long because I truly don't care. When guys got ejected or suspended for going at me in my rookie season, we were all good the next time I saw them. But if you go after one of my Thunder brothers, I'll remember, and I'll be keeping an eye out. I'm like Arya Stark with her list on *Game of Thrones*. Except I'm also Khal Drogo. It's a weird hybrid but I make it work. I'm sure every one of my teammates would be exactly the same in that respect, so even though I wasn't bothered by the whole thing, I knew they'd be mad. But we all knew better than to get distracted by petty feuds being blown up in the media and we just concentrated on game four.

Game four at Oklahoma City

In the very first possession of the game, Draymond fouled me with a hack on my bad hand. The pain and trembling came back, and I knew it was going to be a long game. Four minutes in and I continued my own battering by rolling my right ankle on a rebound attempt. I made my way back to the locker room to get it looked at while our second unit got on court and kept building the lead. When I returned 10 minutes later, we had a 12-point lead. I subbed back in, albeit a bit gingerly, and got back into the groove by sinking a jump hook with my first touch of the ball.

One quarter can change the whole game. In game four, outscoring the Warriors 42–27 in the second quarter changed the game. Good defense leads to good offense and we were playing our best defense. Nothing new, just plain hustle and scrambling for every loose ball. It helped that the Warriors were missing open layups and free throws that they didn't usually miss.

We still had the momentum from our big win in game three, and we used it to get another big win in game four. People didn't know what to say. It was the first time all season that the

Warriors had lost back-to-back games, and everyone was wondering if maybe they were unraveling. We knew not to take our series advantage for granted, but a 3–1 lead was a bloody good position to be in.

We may have won game four, but the real winner that day was "Lil Stache Bro." The "Stache Brothers" were me and Enes. Back in November I told Enes we should get rid of our beards and just rock some mos for a while. He didn't like the idea at first, but I kept nagging him and he finally agreed. Pretty soon people were calling us the "Stache Brothers" and that's when Enes really got into it. He got us T-shirts with our faces on them and we had a caricature done like we were a romantic couple. It was cute. A grooming company even sent us product to keep our upper lips looking fresh. We were both silly and didn't take ourselves too seriously—and the fans loved having something new to put on their signs. Then someone took it to the next level and introduced a "Lil Stache Bro."

A Thunder fan brought their toddler daughter to the game and dressed her up like me. She had her hair done the same and a little mustache. She even had the tattoos on her arm. It was some of the best cosplay I'd ever seen. I never thought I'd be flattered by being compared to a little girl, but she looked fly as hell. In fact, she looked way cooler with a mustache than either of us did, but I'm not bitter about it.

Game five at Golden State

We were one game away from going to the finals. Forty-eight minutes of basketball and we could be conference champions, playing for the championship against the Cavaliers or the Toronto Raptors. We knew the Warriors would come out and throw everything at us. They had home advantage again and a whole new atmosphere to work with.

We had been told we weren't great at closing out games during the regular season, and we had proved everyone wrong so far during the playoffs. It was just a matter of closing out one last game. It would be the biggest upset in years, but it wouldn't be the NBA without a few upsets.

I got hit with two off-ball foul calls within three minutes and had to sit down. I wasn't in the habit of contesting foul calls at that point in my career, but even I knew that a guy running into me and flopping before the play was even set up was a cheap foul to call. I was annoyed at the ref for calling it, but more annoyed at myself for not anticipating a sneaky move like that.

We led only once the whole game and it was by a single point. But even though the Warriors held the lead for basically the whole game, we were never out of it as in previous contests. Anytime they pushed the lead out, we went on a run and closed the gap.

In the two previous games we had outscored them heavily in the paint, and in game five our paint scoring dropped significantly. I couldn't help but think if I hadn't got those two fouls and had to sit out most of the first quarter, I could have changed that.

We never once backed down in that game, despite the series lead we had. They had the desperation, though, and desperation counts for a lot. We took the loss, 120–111, and immediately put it behind us as we headed home.

Game six at Oklahoma City

We were still one game away from the finals. Forget game five. It may as well not have happened. Why dwell on that result when we had game six to win? We were confident. We had home advantage again and hadn't lost at home that series. Game six was our best shot at closing out the series. Having to go back to Golden State for a game seven decider wouldn't work in our favor so we knew tonight was the night to finish it.

By game six, both teams know exactly what they need to do; it's just a matter of executing it consistently. We knew we had to just play our own game on offense and run transition. And on defense it was all about shutting down Curry and Thompson on the perimeter. They had both shot ridiculously well through-out the regular season and so far in the series we'd managed to keep their three-point shooting at a tolerable level. That's all there was to it.

We had our game plan and we executed our game plan. Everyone was doing exactly what the team needed. Russ was driving through everyone for easy buckets, Dre was swatting shots all over the place, the only thing we weren't doing was making threes. But it didn't matter so much because neither were the Warriors. Thompson, known for his three-point shoot-ing, couldn't get anything to drop. The game was being played within the perimeter and that's exactly where we had the advan-tage. Like the Warriors in game five, we led for most of the game.

Chapter three in the supposed feud between Draymond and me unfolded in the second quarter when I dunked on him. It was a standard pick-and-roll and I saw the lane open, so I left the ground to dunk. While I was in the air, he flew in from the side and made contact. I was already in the air and once this body gets moving it's hard to stop it. I finished the dunk and only noticed afterwards that it was Draymond who was under me.

I'd be lying if I said I wasn't a little bit satisfied. All the fans who had bravely cursed Draymond for his kicks to my balls were certainly satisfied.

As we went into the locker room at halftime, we weren't shooting well. But we were hustling and keeping the lead so it wasn't all bad. We knew that whichever team could get their shot to go would have the advantage for the rest of the game. Twenty-four minutes away from going to the finals.

Straight after halftime the Warriors crept back to within one point and then took the lead. Our home crowd sat down for the first time in the series. Billy didn't call a timeout and let us handle it ourselves. We got our heads back in the game thanks to Russ being aggressive in the paint and drawing fouls. I followed Russ's lead and made sure to go up strong in the paint every time. I ended up converting an and-one basket to put us up by eight. After the Warriors' short burst at the beginning of the quarter, we had gotten our groove back and maintained our eight-point lead going into the fourth.

Twelve minutes away from going to the finals. Our lead held steady for the first six minutes. We were still outplaying them in the paint, but they were hanging on thanks to Thompson making a few quick threes in a row. We were doing everything right. Keeping them out of the paint, not letting them get any second shots, and frustrating their bigs enough for Bogut and Draymond to give up fouls and push us into the bonus early.

Five minutes away from going to the finals. Up by eight points and having had the lead for most of the game, our winning probability was at 86 percent. If you're an NBA fan you already know what happened next. Klay Thompson kept shooting. And it felt like he couldn't miss. The Warriors we'd been expecting from game one, but hadn't really seen, finally showed up in the fourth quarter of game six. Curry and Thompson were draining threes from all over the court. I was transported back to my first regional game with the Wellington rep team when we lost to Hawke's Bay. Sometimes a team shoots the lights out and there's not a whole lot you can do. What we definitely could have done was not crumble in the final three minutes.

With two minutes to go, my lungs felt like shriveled prunes, my legs were barely working, and the game was tied at 101–101. After having authority the whole game, we had three turnovers in one minute and Thompson dropped his eleventh three-pointer, a new playoffs record: 104–101.

With 45 seconds left, Thompson finally missed and we got the rebound, then turned it over a second later. The Warriors won game six. They converted 21 three-pointers from 45 attempts. We converted three from 23 and had five turnovers in the final two minutes. We had choked.

We were still one game away from going to the finals.

Game seven at Golden State

It was quiet in the locker room after game six. The veterans on our team said what they could to keep things positive, but we all knew we had blown our best shot. A 3–1 series lead had turned into a game seven decider, with the Warriors having home advantage. Our one positive note was knowing that we had beaten the Warriors at home in game one, so we'd been there before. But the Warriors had torn away the momentum and that last five minutes had passed a huge advantage from us to them.

Game seven was messy. Desperation will do that to a man, no matter how much money he's making. I kept busy in the opening minutes, taking shots, getting rebounds, and, sadly, guarding Steph Curry on the perimeter. He and Thompson were shooting well again, but so were we. After making a total of three three-pointers in game six, we made three in the first six minutes of game seven.

To no one's surprise, Draymond Green and I got into it again. Going up for a rebound, he fell back and took my arm with him. I was flipped over and ended up on my back on top of him. I knew I didn't do anything, but while the refs reviewed it for a long time the crowd started chanting, "Throw him out! Throw him out!" I figured they probably wouldn't be yelling that about their own guy, which meant they were wanting me kicked out. The refs ended up calling it a double foul, meaning no one was happy about it. At that point we had an 11-point lead, so I focused on that instead.

If we faltered in game six in the last five minutes, we did the same in game seven in the third quarter. We kept doing the work in the paint, but the Warriors had moved the game to beyond the perimeter, where they lived. Because of how much their system moved off the ball, I found myself guarding Curry and Thompson on the perimeter again and again. My reach did nothing to stop their threes from going in. But for some reason all our threes stopped dropping. Our 13-point lead in the second quarter turned into an 11-point deficit by the end of the third.

We had a lot of work to do in the fourth quarter if we wanted to keep our season alive. We finally dropped some more threes and cut the lead down to five. As KD shot one of them, I set a screen and rolled the opposite way, blocking Andre Iguodala. When I turned back around on defense he looked mad, and I had a feeling we'd be getting into it again on the next play. But instead I was given a rest. My last play of the 2016 season was setting a screen for KD. Strangely poetic when I look back on it now.

The Warriors held on to their lead and kept us at arm's length for the remaining few minutes. We had blown a 3–1 series lead. Our season was finished.

After the game, with the sound of the celebrating Warriors' fans rippling its way through the corridors and into our locker room, we said nothing. There was nothing to say. We all knew we should have won that series two games earlier and deserved to be in the finals. No one spoke about getting redemption next year because of course we were getting redemption next year.

We were going to have a sour taste in our mouths all summer because of that series and we weren't planning to have sour mouths for any longer than that. There was unfinished business to attend to as soon as we were back in OKC after the break. No one needed convincing.

At least that's what I thought.

16.

MR. TRIPLE-DOUBLE

"MVP! MVP! MVP!"

The chant was deafening—the closest you could get to a playoff atmosphere during the regular season. The crowd, who had been largely quiet for most of the game, were now chanting for Russ as he took two free throws in the fourth quarter against the Denver Nuggets. MVP chants had been a regular occurrence at home games in the lead-up to the playoffs, and this was no different. Except it was, because we weren't playing at home. Russ was getting MVP chants from the Nuggets' home crowd in the middle of a tight fourth quarter.

They weren't chanting for nothing. In fact, I'd come to accept Denver as being one of the toughest places to play because of the altitude and their aggressive fans. But even the bitterest of fans can appreciate being a part of history as it's unfolding.

With three games left to play, Russ had recorded 41 triple-doubles and was sitting equal with Oscar Robertson for the most triple-doubles in a regular season. Two days earlier, against the Atlanta Hawks, he became the second player in history (after Robertson) to average a triple-double throughout an NBA regular season. At that point it was clear to everyone that the season belonged to Russ and we were just there for the ride.

We all knew he would get that last triple-double, but we were hoping he wouldn't leave it to the last game. The Denver altitude meant that even though everyone was fit, it was always a bitch to play there and I never felt 100 percent in that arena. Not Russ, though; he played the same as always. That's because Russell Westbrook approaches every game the same, as anyone who has ever seen an interview with him will know.

After the series loss to the Warriors, no one expected Russ to have to carry our team in the new season. In fact, no one was expecting anything to change at all. Players move between teams and pretty much all of that stuff happens behind closed doors, but we knew we had a championship team. Why mess with it? But of course that's when KD left to join the very organization that had just beaten us.

OKC TEAM ROSTER 2016–17

ALEX ABRINES, guard

STEVEN ADAMS, center

SEMAJ CHRISTON, guard

NORRIS COLE, guard

NICK COLLISON, forward

TAJ GIBSON, forward

JERAMI GRANT, forward

JOSH HUESTIS, forward

ENES KANTER, center

DOUG MCDERMOTT, forward

VICTOR OLADIPO, guard

ANDRE "DRE" ROBERSON, guard

DOMANTAS SABONIS, center

KYLE SINGLER, forward

RUSSELL "RUSS" WESTBROOK, guard

Like everyone else in the team, I found out that KD had left by looking at my phone. I think Nick sent a message in the group chat. Everyone was shocked. We had all gone our separate ways to get some space to reflect on what was an intense postseason, but I never once thought about whether any players would leave. I was in New Zealand paintballing with a bunch of old mates when the news came through. I hadn't really been keeping in touch with any of the Thunder crew, because the first month of the off-season is log-off mode when you don't have to think about basketball so much. I took that month very seriously and used it to relax at home and remember that basketball isn't everything.

I understood why KD did what he did, although I might have done it differently. Winning a championship ring is more important to some players than others. For me, as long as I can keep improving and developing as a player, I'm happy. And it helps when I know I'm surrounded by good people who feel the same. Plus, I couldn't handle the snake comments.

> Russ got his ninth assist with two minutes to go in the third quarter. He already had over 30 points and a dozen rebounds, and now he just needed one more assist for that triple-double. The crowd knew what was going on and every time he made a pass there was a collective gasp as everyone waited for a shot. Meanwhile, I was on the bench. It was the end of the season and our playoff spot was safe at sixth seed.

I was a bit bummed for a day about KD and then I got back to enjoying my off-season. Without having to play in the Summer

League I was able to spend more time in New Zealand and traveling. And the main reason I love doing those things is the food.

Oklahoma City is great and the people are awesome, but it doesn't have the food that New Zealand has. Whenever I bring Thunder guys over for my camps, I make sure they try all the food we have, including the traditional hāngī, which is the bomb.

I think part of the reason I love it so much is that it's a family thing. You can't just go out and decide to do a hāngī by yourself one afternoon. It takes hours of preparation. Digging the hole, heating the stones, getting all the food wrapped up tight, putting the food on the hot stones, and filling up the hole with dirt. Then you wait as it cooks for hours underground before pulling it back up and serving. I like to do it with my brothers and their families and it becomes like a mini reunion anytime we have a hāngī.

That's why food is such a big part of my life. It comes with cultural and family significance, and I like to show my Thunder family what it's all about.

New Zealand is so, so multicultural, and you can find food from any country made by people from that country. My go-to whenever I am home is R & S Satay Noodle House on Cuba Street in Wellington. If you're ever in Wellington, go there and get the chicken noodle soup. It will make you question your own mum's cooking.

Other than food, I always try to show the OKC guys how beautiful New Zealand is. It's not that there aren't beautiful places in America, it's just that New Zealand is better. When Nick and Dre came over for the camps after our series loss to the Warriors, we went on a classic Kiwi roadie. I wanted to show them what I did for fun, which was eat, hang out on farms, and wear Swanndries. They got into it and I wasn't surprised when Dre said he wanted to come back again the next year. I'm sure he wants to buy a farm down south and retire there. I don't blame him.

> Russ rested for the end of the third quarter and the start of the fourth. That's what was crazy. He was averaging a triple-double but wasn't even playing whole games. The Nuggets were up by 10, but our second unit was doing well to keep them within reach. As soon as Russ got back in, everyone knew we were gonna get him that assist. Haters loved to say that Russ's teammates helped him get his triple-doubles by gifting rebounds, but it was funny how no one else in the league was performing anywhere close to him all season. Were their teammates not nice enough or something? As soon as Russ got on the floor he passed to Enes for a layup, but Enes traveled. No deal.

The trip around New Zealand was fun but more importantly it gave Nick, Dre, and me time together away from basketball to chill out before we returned to OKC and to our new, bigger roles in the Thunder organization. With KD signing with the Warriors and Serge traded to the Magic, suddenly Dre and I were Thunder veterans. Only Russ and Nick had been there longer than us, and we were just entering our fourth season.

We began the off-season expecting to win the championship

with the same team the next season, and we ended it with a brand-new squad and brand-new roles. That's the business of basketball. The one steady ship in all of it was Russ, who had just signed a three-year extension and put everyone at ease. I knew Russ wasn't going anywhere, but it was good to have it confirmed.

> Pretty soon, every time Russ got the ball, the Denver crowd would stand up and cheer with their phones ready to record the historic moment. The problem was, he needed one of his teammates to actually score off his pass. And mate, we were not on form.

Once again, I found myself elevated to a position I hadn't thought I would reach for a few more years. But I didn't stress about it because my track record showed I did better when thrust into challenging roles. Just last season I had recorded six double-doubles all regular season and then recorded six double-doubles during the playoffs. I liked being put under pressure and I was about to get a whole lot of it.

In our first game of the preseason, it was buzzy to see myself next to Russ on all the graphics around the arena. Before it had been Russ and KD, or Russ, KD, and Serge. I had had the luxury of not having to look at myself everywhere. Now it was just Russ left from that group. I'd gone from a supposedly risky draft pick to the billboards of a playoff team in three years. I don't think anybody predicted that, least of all me. Being the vets on the team, suddenly my pick-and-roll with Russ became one of the most used plays in our arsenal. My workload in the paint felt like it doubled, even though I was still doing the same things.

> With each shot that we missed off Russ's passes,
> the groans from the crowd got louder. How
> hard could it be for someone other than Russ to
> score? Enes missed, Domantas Sabonis missed,
> Domantas missed again and the crowd were
> getting rowdy. All this missing meant the Nuggets'
> lead stretched out to 14. So the next time we came
> down the court, Russ pulled up and nailed a three
> from the top of the key. He would rather win than
> get the triple-double.

As I became more and more central to the team and its success, I distanced myself from social media. When I was a rookie I wanted to know what everyone thought, and I was open to advice from anyone. But after a season of trying to please or impress strangers on the internet, I realized I had to stop or it would ruin me. I'll be honest, in the beginning the attention was intoxicating. Thousands of people were genuinely interested in everything I was doing and part of me loved it. But after a while I knew that if I got too hooked on people saying nice things about me, I wouldn't be able to handle when they said nasty things, which was bound to happen. I drifted away from social media and put that energy into my team.

Being on social media too much also meant I was closer and closer to being part of the drama. Some teams love drama, but the Thunder like to keep things chill.

> Even though we were playing away from home,
> there was a pocket of loyal Thunder fans sitting not
> far from our bench. Honestly, they were louder than

the whole rest of the stadium. Everyone was still standing, waiting for that tenth assist, and it was becoming like a block. No one could concentrate while history was still on the line.

I was still one of the younger guys in the team, but age doesn't mean much in sport. You're either a leader or you're not. I was about to find out which label I held. We got Victor Oladipo in the Serge trade, and it was nice to see a familiar face. Victor had been the second overall pick in my draft year so Dre and I had gotten to know him at rookie events before our first season. He could sing, which was a problem because I had already established myself as the best shower singer in the team. Except he could *really* sing and sang all the time, so Russ and I became his back-up vocalists.

> With a few minutes left in the game, Russ drove to the hoop and passed out to Semaj Christon for a baseline three. That shot was recorded by thousands of Denver fans as it went in and the place erupted. Russell Westbrook was the new record holder for the most triple-doubles in a regular season. I'm sure the Denver fans cheered extra loud because they were still up by 10 and thought they had the game in the bag.

Predictably, our season wasn't as good as the one before. We intended to be competitors and make the playoffs, which we did, but it was also a rebuilding season. For years our team had been built around Russ and KD. I was happy being a role player and I would have been happy staying a role player my whole career.

But that's not what the Thunder front office had in mind when my rookie contract ran out.

> I subbed back in on the next play as the MVP chants started and Russ got back to being a scoring machine. He may have just made history, but we still had a lead to cut and a game to win. Ten points is nothing in an NBA game and we had at least two minutes.

Once you've been in the NBA a few years you start to think that your life is normal. You can start to think that being paid $2 million a year isn't a lot because it's not a lot in the NBA. So when contracts run out and negotiations for extensions start to happen, it's easy to lose sight of the real world and what's normal there.

After my rookie year I signed a three-year extension and that extension was going to run out at the end of the 2016–17 season, making me a restricted free agent. Restricted free agency means a player can sign an offer sheet from any team, but their original team is allowed to match that deal and essentially have first dibs. To avoid all of this, teams that want to keep their players will sort out an extension well before the player enters free agency.

The Thunder were keen to keep me around so in the summer before the 2016–17 season, they started working on a contract extension. I wasn't involved in the talks—that's what agents are for—but I knew they were wanting to work out a deal and I was happy to hear it. The NBA is a fickle business and players get traded at the snap of a finger. I'll always remember being on the bus heading to the stadium in Golden State and sitting next to

Lance Thomas, one of my buddies. I had my headphones on like everyone else and it wasn't until I got inside the arena that I realized Lance wasn't around. "Where's Lance?" I asked one of the trainers. He looked at me as if I was messing with him. When he saw I wasn't, he replied, "Didn't you hear? He got traded to the Knicks." Lance's trade had been finalized while we were on the bus and, because he was now officially a Knick, he wasn't even allowed inside. He waited on the bus and was taken back to the hotel. That's the business of basketball.

I felt lucky to be with an organization that wanted to extend my contract because I loved playing for the Thunder, and frankly it sounded like a real hassle to move to a new city and new team. At some point in the talks I was told to say what I thought I was worth—a dollar amount that I thought I deserved to be paid. Have you ever had to answer that question? I'll tell you right now, it's not an easy one to answer. If I was talking about working out a contract for virtually any job in the real world, I would not answer that question with $100 million. But the NBA is not the real world, it's a world where answering that question with $100 million is a perfectly reasonable thing to do. In fact, it's so reasonable that the Thunder front office agreed with me.

> With less than two minutes to go and down by five, I got called for two off-ball fouls in the space of 15 seconds. Usually it was me managing to get sneaky fouls out of opponents, but Nikola Jokic gave me a taste of my own medicine that night. The next time Russ got to the foul line, the MVP chants were long gone and the boos were back.

I signed my contract extension in November 2016. Four years and $100 million. It was a massive deal, but not because of the money. It was massive because it meant I would have a job for at least another four years and the chance to achieve big things with the Thunder.

> Russ scored easily yet again and we were within two points with two possessions left in the game. We needed a stop and a basket. The Nuggets wound down as much of the clock as they could before taking a shot. They missed, Russ snatched a clutch rebound and called a timeout. We had 2.9 seconds to score a field goal to tie, or a three-pointer to win. Russ wanted the win.

When you sign a $100 million contract, people want to see $100 million plays immediately. My contract wouldn't begin till the next season, but that didn't matter. I was now the guy getting paid more than half the league's superstars (only because their old contracts hadn't ended yet) and fans wanted me to prove it somehow. All I knew how to do was to keep playing how I'd always played—tough.

Perhaps my new signing was a boost to my confidence because I decided to properly respond to trash talk for the first and last time. Jonas Valanciunas from the Raptors was ripping into me all game, totally aggro. When he asked for a fight for the hundredth time, I finally turned to him and said, "You don't want to mess with me. You use a knife and fork to eat your food. I use my hands." He didn't know how to respond to that because it was so dumb, but it got him to shut up for a while, so I guess it worked. I decided to retire from trash talking after that game and go out on a win.

> The inbound play was designed for me to set a screen for Russ at the top of the key so he could get the pass and shoot straight away. But when he cut off my shoulder, his defender stayed right with him and he couldn't get the pass. So I turned, was open and ended up with the ball. There were only two seconds on the clock, but I knew there was no way in hell that ball was leaving my hands in the direction of the hoop. Instead, I looked for Russ, who was now a good 10 feet beyond the perimeter, and chucked him the ball. He caught it and shot it from way downtown with a defender right on him.

Our season had been bumpy, we were young and new, but Russ put us all on his back. We all had to step up and most of us did, but probably not as much as we wanted to. Russ still had to shoulder the vast majority of the media scrutiny and, as any NBA fan will know, Russ doesn't like to chat all that much when it's for media. But he still went out of his way to take responsibility for our team after every game and not let the rest of us be blindsided by a question from the press. Off the court, Russ was a bit of a goof, but on paper he kept things short.

Everyone had said Russ would have to have a big season for us to make the playoffs. No one said he would have to have one of the greatest seasons in NBA history. But he did it anyway, because that's what Russ does.

The shot looked good. It looked even better when it dropped through the net while the buzzer was still sounding. We won 106–105. On the day Russ got his record-breaking forty-second triple-double, he scored 50 points and won the game with a buzzer-beater three-pointer.

If there was any doubt he would win MVP that year, it was erased after the Denver game. When the shot dropped, the bench jumped up and ran on court to embrace him. Even the Denver crowd, whose team had just been eliminated from playoff contention, couldn't help but cheer for him. He had just capped off one of the greatest individual regular seasons in NBA history, but it was clear that we weren't a title contender. We needed more firepower. And we got it just three months later.

17.

THE COMPLETE THOUGHTS OF RUSSELL WESTBROOK ON HIS GOOD FRIEND AND TEAMMATE STEVEN ADAMS

"He's great."

18.

THE NEW BIG THREE

The drama of the NBA goes way beyond the court. Even when the season is over, fans obsess over the trades. And that's how it was in September 2017.

We had made the playoffs in April, which surprised a few people. But we lost 4–1 to the Houston Rockets in the first round. It had been a long season with everyone on the team having more responsibility than they had ever had before. While we thought we'd done well, we knew the front office would be looking to make some big trades over the summer.

If my job was to get better as a player every day, the general manager's job was to put together a team that could win a championship. I don't think anyone was operating under the delusion that our current setup would win a championship. Something had to change. And a lot of things did in September.

The day my "Stache Brother" was taken from me was a rest day. But of course Russ, Dre, and I were in the gym having a workout.

I knew there was a trade in the works because every front-office worker in the facility was making phone calls all morning. A tiny part of me thought maybe I was about to be traded. Columnist and blogger Bill Simmons had tweeted earlier in the week that the Knicks were looking to trade Kristaps Porzingis and were in talks with the Thunder. Kristaps is a center so people assumed if a trade happened, I would be the one to go. Then articles were written saying I was probably going to be traded to the Knicks by the end of the week. It was all bullshit and a rumor that started from one tweet that never even mentioned my name, but that's how crazy NBA fans get during trade season.

Instead we found out that Enes and Doug McDermott had been traded to the Knicks in exchange for Carmelo Anthony. I was gutted. Not about the Melo part (Melo's the man) but that my buddy Enes, who just days earlier had made a video about how much he loved Oklahoma, was leaving.

We went straight to see Enes at another gym where he was holding a basketball camp for some of the local kids. It was really fitting that on the day he was traded, Enes was giving back to the community. We crashed his camp and let him know that he would always be our bro. That night, Russ and I took him out to dinner for his final night in OKC before he flew to New York.

That's how it goes with basketball. You can be completely at home and happy in one city then living in another one the next day. I had just bought a home in OKC so was pretty glad not to have to move again. It's hard because you want to settle in and make a city your home, but at the same time you really can be traded at any moment and there's nothing you can do. It can be brutal.

OKC TEAM ROSTER 2017–18

ALEX ABRINES, guard

STEVEN ADAMS, center

CARMELO "MELO" ANTHONY, forward

COREY BREWER, guard

NICK COLLISON, forward

P. J. DOZIER, guard

RAYMOND FELTON, guard

TERRANCE FERGUSON, guard

PAUL "PG" GEORGE, forward

JERAMI GRANT, forward

DANIEL HAMILTON, guard

JOSH HUESTIS, forward

DAKARI JOHNSON, center

PATRICK PATTERSON, forward

ANDRE "DRE" ROBERSON, guard

KYLE SINGLER, forward

RUSSELL "RUSS" WESTBROOK, guard

I can't imagine what it's like for those players who have played for 10 different teams in their careers. If it were up to me, I would stay with the Thunder forever and take over from Nick as the oldest guy on the team.

There's definitely a double standard in the NBA around trades. When a team trades a beloved player to another organization, most of the time people just consider it a business decision. Too bad for the player; that's the nature of the league. But when a player chooses to join a new team, they are labeled a traitor and greedy and all sorts of bad things. What's the difference? We're all here trying to win. That's why teams trade players and that's why players sign with new teams. It's all the same, and yet players are expected to be loyal to one team while also being shipped around endlessly if GMs decide they don't need them anymore.

I was happy for Enes, though. New York is the perfect place for him. They go hard and don't hold back on anything, which is exactly Enes's style. As soon as he landed in New York City he started stirring shit and starting beef with everyone. I loved it.

At the Thunder we like to keep a low profile and keep our guys out of social media spats, but the Knicks fans love it when Enes goes in fighting for them. He's had beef with LeBron James, with people saying he's all talk and would pussy out of a fight. Last I knew, Enes was wanted for arrest in his home country of Turkey for talking shit about their *president*. So, no, Enes wouldn't back out of a confrontation with LeBron James. But, yes, he would definitely get knocked out because he can't fight for shit.

Enes got traded, Doug got traded, Victor Oladipo got traded,

Domantas Sabonis got traded. We lost a lot of good guys that summer. But we got Melo and Paul George ("PG"), and Russ signed a five-year contract extension. Suddenly, our team looked like a super team and was being hyped as one.

I was happy to go back to my more defined role in the paint and leave the new big three to work out the rest. That's what they were called. First the "Big Three" and then the "OKC Three" and sometimes the "OK3." Russ, PG, and Melo. They were the new faces of the Thunder and, honestly, I was so glad. Some fans insisted that I should be included in the new nicknames, but I was happy working in the shadows. I'd be completely invisible if it helped my team win games.

During that same off-season, while the Thunder front office were furiously negotiating trades all over the place, New Zealand was working on its own recruit. *Will Steven Adams play for the Tall Blacks this year?* This question has been asked every year since I declared for the draft and every year I have the same answer. "Today, no. Some day, yes." Every time the question comes up, a lot of people don't get my position. In most sports, representing New Zealand in a black singlet is the peak. Athletics, netball, rowing... But there are some sports, such as soccer, tennis, and basketball, where playing overseas is the ultimate goal. That's the pinnacle of those sports.

Yes, I would love to represent New Zealand by playing for the Tall Blacks, but right now I don't feel I have time to give it my best and play a full NBA season. It probably doesn't help that I don't feel a great sense of loyalty to Basketball New Zealand. I like what the current Tall Blacks coach, Paul Henare, has been doing with the team and I would love to play for him at some point, but I need to be ready.

Some might expect me to be the Basketball New Zealand poster child, but I did the opposite of rising through the ranks of junior national teams. Being in a national team is far too expensive for most kids—me included. Kenny set up the alternate route, the New Zealand Basketball Academy, which runs free trainings every morning in Wellington and sends teams to Las Vegas every year for their annual tournament. Those Vegas trips are expensive too, but the difference is that the community comes together to support the players. Teams now have their own Debbies and Bernices as team managers who tirelessly navigate fundraising with the players. If they need a bit of help to make their target, I'll also pitch in so they can go.

It takes a village to raise a child, apparently. And it takes a village to fundraise for one too. New Zealand does best when everyone is invested. I had my own little community of helpers who pushed me towards my passion, but that's not a cost-effective approach. Kenny still takes every morning training, like he has for over a decade, and I know there will be plenty more basketballers thanking him for their success in years to come. But, for now, his project from 2008 has one focus and that focus is the Thunder and the NBA.

The 2017–18 season was a bumpy one. We had never had big names like PG and Melo join our team before, and it took a few months for everyone to figure out what their role in the squad was and how they could best help us win. We worked hard on it because we knew that with the guys we had, a championship ring was there for the taking. But the same could be said of a handful of other teams. It all comes down to who can do it on the day.

NBA analysts called 2017–18 my breakout season. Before Christmas I had my best offensive game ever against the Minnesota Timberwolves with 27 points from a perfect shooting game, 11 from 11 and five from five free throws. Apparently, I joined a couple of old guys as the only players to go 11 from 11 in a game in NBA history. That was cool.

That same game I busted out the Euro step for the first time—pretty much a rugby sidestep but done slower. I scooped up the ball at half court on transition and realized there was no one in front to pass to so I dribbled (rare) and went for the fast break Euro step (unheard of). I made the basket and I swear I heard my teammates cracking up from the bench.

The truth is, I wasn't playing any different from how I played the season before. The difference was that we had three All-Star scoring threats on the perimeter, which draws out the defense and gives me plenty of room to work and score inside the paint. If I had a good game, it's because my teammates were shooting well and forcing my defenders out to focus on them, leaving me with more open looks.

I liked how our team looked. Everyone bought in 100 percent and committed to the cause. We went on a winning streak and then followed that with a losing streak. But it's the adversity that made us a tighter unit and forced us to understand each other better both on and off the court. When we didn't play well, we all wanted to figure out why. To do that means spending more time with each other off the court, eating out after a game or having dinner at someone's house (I pretty much don't do anything unless there's food involved).

I was thrust into a leadership role at the end of 2016 that accelerated my growth within the organization, but the 2017–18 season allowed me to get back to being a defensive anchor and role player. I still did what I could to help the newer players on the team, but there were more senior players all of a sudden, which translated into huge improvements in my game.

When I began as a rookie with the Thunder, I did my work, played hard, and made sure not to talk to the refs in case I got a technical foul. When a call didn't go my way, I knew that Russ would be right there, asking the ref to explain it. That's what leaders do for their teammates.

Even in the 2016–17 season, when it was usually Russ and me sitting down for the press conference after games, Russ was still the leader. When a reporter asked how the rest of us played without Russ on the court, Russ stepped in and told him not to try to separate our team. We won as a team and we lost as a team, even if Russ was topping every stat pretty much every game.

Now, we had new guys like Dakari Johnson and Terrance Ferguson who had all the right instincts but didn't always get their way on court. It was then my job to be the one to question the refs and speak up for my boys. Yes, the Thunder is a business and sometimes business can be cruel. You never know who will still be in your team at the end of the season. But once we get a team together, we're brothers. And we'd die for each other.

When Dre got injured playing the Detroit Pistons, that hurt me even more than when I had my own injuries. He went up for an alley-oop and tore his patellar tendon. I'm not entirely sure what that is, but I knew it was bad as soon as he hit the ground. Dre is tough and doesn't stay down unless something is really wrong. When he didn't get up, I sat down with him until the stretcher came in. That's what you do when someone you love is hurt. You stay near them and give them strength through your presence.

Dre and I started our NBA journeys together, and if it were up to either of us we would end them together too. I've eaten a lot of Whole Foods sandwiches with that guy, sitting on the back of my truck in the parking lot, having a yarn. When you've spent five years learning to be adults together, your careers become intertwined. So when Dre went down, I felt like we were both injured. I knew he'd be back, though, because I wouldn't leave him alone until he was.

Dre and I had become the defensive anchors of the team, him up top and me in the paint. And we were proud to be leaders on defense and team hustle. That's what a lot of young players forget. Being a great defender is just as valuable as being able to score, if not more so. Literally anyone can hustle on defense. If you're struggling with your shot or you can't seem to make plays happen, I say work on your defense. Become the best defender in your league and no one will care how many points you score.

The same can be said for setting screens. A strong screen is a massive weapon in the game and about the most contact you can enforce without being pulled up for a foul. If you can set a good screen for your teammate to score, that's basically an assist. And opponents will start to hate you for it. Tough screens have become my specialty and I make sure that everyone thinks twice before running into me. Defense, screening, and rebounding are underappreciated by a lot of kids, but doing those three things well doesn't require inherent talent and will take you places, I promise.

Dre is the best defender I know and when PG joined us, we became *the* defensive team in the NBA. With Dre out for the rest of the season, we all had to adjust and step up to fill the massive hole he left, but it wouldn't be a full NBA season without a few setbacks.

We got into a habit of beating the best teams and losing to the worst teams. It wasn't an ideal situation to be in, but it was comforting to know that only the best teams make the playoffs so statistically we had good odds to go all the way.

Things don't always go to plan, though. We lost to the Utah Jazz in the first round of the playoffs. Our season was over, but I knew we'd be back next season to fight again. No matter the outcome, we never flinch.

19.

WHAT NOW?

In New Zealand I'm part of a brown minority. In the NBA I'm in a white minority. And in Oklahoma City I'm somehow both. No matter where I go I don't seem to fit neatly into a box. Usually it doesn't matter too much and being in the NBA and earning millions of dollars means I don't have to deal with the discrimination some of my family have had to deal with back home. But it also means that for the first time in my life I have to be careful about what I say. I learned this the hard way when thousands of people called me a racist.

In my first few years with the Thunder I didn't have to do too many interviews. We had stars on our team that the media wanted to hear from and I was glad not to have to be in front of the camera after every game. However, when I did end up with a microphone in my face I always tried to really listen to the reporters' questions and answer as honestly as possible. I liked to joke around with them too. We all have jobs to do and the reporters' job is to ask questions, so I tried to make their lives a bit easier by giving interesting answers.

As the seasons went on, I started to play more, and I guess I became known as a good interview because the media began requesting time with me more often. I was still not giving nearly as many interviews as Russ and KD, but more than I was used to. By the time I was the go-to guy with Russ at the end of 2016, I felt like I was spending half my days answering questions. But my one slip-up that got me in trouble came earlier, after game one of the conference finals against the Warriors.

We had just managed an upset win and I had had a good game so was ushered over to Chris Broussard from ESPN. The interview was the usual stuff, talking about sticking to game plans and executing, blah blah blah. Then he finished by asking what it was like for me to sometimes have to guard Steph Curry and Klay Thompson on the perimeter after a pick-and-roll switch. I laughed because we both knew I hated it. I told him I didn't envy guards because "they're quick little monkeys, those guys."

I went back to the locker room, had a shower, and returned to the hotel. Then I checked my phone. Apparently I was a racist. I had to go through quite a few tweets to find what I had said to send people into a spin. When I saw it was the word "monkey" I was honestly just confused.

In New Zealand, parents call their kids "monkeys" all the time. Little rascal, little monkey, they mean the same thing—a naughty kid with too much energy who runs around endlessly. I had no idea that monkey had ever been used as a derogatory term anywhere. After googling it, I learned pretty quickly. My teammates thought it was kind of funny because it was just me being an idiot and not knowing anything. And they gave me a pass because I'm "European white."

In the NBA there are three skin colors—black, American white, and European white. European white means literally anyone who is not from America. It's a classic American move to assume that the rest of the world is all the same, so Tony Parker (French, but born in Belgium, with an African American father and Dutch mother) is European white, Alex Abrines (Spanish) is European white and, apparently, I'm European white as well. I wouldn't have gotten a pass if I were American white, because that would mean I grew up there and should know the history of racial discrimination and derogatory terms. Instead I grew up in New Zealand, where I was used to being the one discriminated against.

Being Tongan and poor, I could basically say whatever I wanted growing up because I was only ever punching up. At Scots College I was one of the only brown students, and definitely one of the only poor students, so I was incapable of saying the wrong thing. People in New Zealand also seemed to care less about what everyone said and whether or not it was offensive.

I'm all for increased awareness and for being more sensitive to everyone's struggles, especially when they are different from your own, but I also know that sometimes people really do just say things out of ignorance and not malice. I did that, my teammates educated me, I apologized, and now I know why what I said was wrong and I won't say it again.

When I made that comment, America was in the middle of a shambles election. The whole country was divided, and it was a little scary seeing how far people went in their political beliefs. I can't vote in America so I wasn't really paying attention, but it was hard to miss what was going on.

Trump's a dick; that's obvious. But Oklahoma is a Republican voting state that backed Trump in the 2016 election. When people attack Trump, they like to attack Republicans too. I don't identify as a Republican, but I understand some of the values they believe in and I also understand that I'm a well-paid NBA basketball player who doesn't have to deal with the effects of policy changes in any real sense.

Some people look at Republican states and lump everyone together, saying they're scum. It's just a state like every other state and there's a whole spectrum of beliefs, so really those who say that are the scum for being narrow-minded about it. I probably shouldn't be saying anything about U.S. politics except be nice to each other.

I did vote in the New Zealand election in 2017. I didn't even know one was happening until I went back home in the off-season and saw all the campaign billboards around. While I knew all about U.S. politics without even wanting to, I didn't know anything about the New Zealand election. I had gone to the Beehive once to meet Prime Minister John Key. He was nice, but I have no idea if he was a good prime minister.

I wanted to vote in New Zealand, but I hadn't read up enough on each of the candidates. In the end I voted for Gareth Morgan's The Opportunities Party because he had a lisp and a decent mustache. Then I heard that after the election he was mean about the new prime minister's cat dying and that's not cool. I'd like to formally retract my vote, thanks.

That's the weird thing about elections. They make you realize which part of society you belong in. Most of the time it's either a race thing, a money thing, or an age thing. But during the New

Zealand elections I realized that I didn't belong in the categories I thought I did. I still think of myself as a poor brown kid from Rotorua. I don't dress any differently than I did 10 years ago. I'll still walk around the Thunder gym and out in the parking lot barefoot because I didn't wear shoes for most of my childhood.

I wear my clothes until I have to throw them out because they're too gross. I bought a camo jacket, like, two seasons ago and I'm still wearing that thing almost every day, to trainings and games and back in New Zealand. There was actually an NBA rule that players weren't allowed to wear sweats or to dress too casual before games. I always wore the closest thing I could to sweatpants without getting fined. Then last year they got rid of that rule and I've been living the life of game-night tracksuits and camo gears ever since.

At first Dre and Russ tried to get me to wear nicer clothes to games. They said I was bringing down the style of the team. But now they embrace it. They know it's my own unique style and they let me do my thing. My point is, I don't feel like I've changed, even though to everyone else it probably seems like I've changed a lot.

It's been a learning curve going from poor and brown to rich and white (according to the NBA and its fans), but I'm doing my best to use my new privilege for good. We do a lot of cool community stuff with the Thunder. The Thunder organization has one of the biggest community presences of all the NBA teams, which is something we're all really proud of.

As a rookie, one of the responsibilities you have is going out and doing things in the community. Sometimes it's giving out books from the book bus or reading to kids at a school, or having Thanksgiving lunch with a foster home. It's all fun stuff because the kids are always awesome, but it took me a few years to realize that my presence could be inspiring for kids.

At first, I almost felt bad that they had to have the guy who sits on the bench most games, instead of them getting to see someone like Russ. I soon realized that they love all the Thunder guys and me being there was a thrill for them. Once I learned that, I made sure to be their favorite Thunder player by the time I left.

Outside of our team efforts, the front office always encourages and supports our own individual ventures. Russ has his Why Not? Foundation, I have my camps in New Zealand, Enes held camps in OKC. Almost every player has their own things they do to try to pay it forward.

Paying it forward is what I like doing. When I say that, I mean giving a leg up to people who are doing everything they can but could do with some support. There's not a single successful person who didn't get help from a bunch of people along the way. But I know that most of the people who helped me did so because they wanted to, not because they thought they might be rewarded later. When I made it to the NBA, those same people were so happy for me and proud to have been a part of my journey. Now I want to be that person for a bunch of other kids. It's human nature to help others, and now that I have money and some influence, I want to use it to help as many people as possible.

My family don't care what I do or how successful I am. Now they are just happy to see me when I'm home. My older brother Rob still insists on paying for every meal we have together because that's what big brothers do. It sounds kind of silly, but I love it when he does that because it's one of the few times in my life these days when I get looked after in that way.

I believe there's a sense of pride in doing as much as you can on your own. I know that if someone in my family bought me something and said it was payback for something I'd done for them years ago, I'd feel 100 percent disrespected. And I think it's the same with them too. We want to fight our own fights, not get handouts.

I got a lot of help from people because they could see that I was fighting. I was getting up every morning and working to be better. And they helped me out because I was helping myself. That's why I put on my camps and make sure everyone's fed and try to get people connected with the right coaches. If I can see that kids are fighting and trying to be better, I'll do whatever I can to help them along.

So, no, I haven't bought everyone I know a new house or a new car or anything like that. But when a young player needs new shoes or can't afford stationery or a basketball trip, that's when I'm willing to spend my money.

After my second season in the NBA, I set up a scholarship with Scots College. It would be a full scholarship given to a promising basketball player. I told Kenny to pick the player he thought would get the most out of it, and we agreed it wouldn't be an annual thing. Instead, Kenny would let me know each year if he had a big talent who would get a lot of help at Scots and I would pay their tuition and any other fees. Again, I didn't want to throw money at something just for the sake of it, I wanted to make sure that I was supporting someone who was really working hard and trying to be the best.

It's a responsibility I feel as someone with fame and fortune. The best thing about being well known is having a platform you can use to draw attention to worthy causes. I held a charity golf tournament the last time I was in New Zealand to try to get others who have wealth to put it towards helping those who don't.

All my focus at the moment is on getting kids into school and sports, regardless of the social barriers, because that is effectively what saved my life when I was young. But I care about a lot of issues, and in the future I'm sure I'll be using my platform to speak out on those. For now, I stick to what I really know, which is sport.

I know that being famous doesn't mean I should be allowed a voice on every topic. There's a reason people need qualifications. Yes, NBA players have influence and are important voices when it comes to speaking on social injustices. But at the same time some of us can't even agree on what shape our planet is so I don't think we deserve the ears of the public all the time.

To me, having a platform and resources is the best thing about my position. The things that fans think are cool, I'm usually not too fussed about. People always want to know what it's like to be paid as much as I'm paid, and what I spend my money on. The truth is, nothing. I don't spend my money on anything. I live by the "enough" rule. I make sure I have enough, and that's it.

Aside from my home, I haven't made any big purchases. At the end of my rookie season I bought two guitars and that was the closest I got to splashing out. I have everything I need to be happy and possessions won't change that. I was happy living in Wellington, wearing the same clothes every day, playing guitar and video games in my spare time, and training as much as I could. Ten years later and I'm pretty much living the same lifestyle. The only difference is I don't have to worry about money, which is a luxury I know a lot of people don't have. I still wear the same clothes and play guitar and video games in my spare time, and train as much as I can. Isn't it everyone's dream to be paid to do what they loved doing as a broke teenager?

Right now, I'm happy. I have a dream job where I get to do what I love every day. I like my teammates, which is a big bonus. I have my own space where I can relax and have fun. But the main reason I'm happy is because I have my fight. My fight is what I call my need to be better all the time. At the moment, my fight is basketball. Every day I wake up and want to be better at basketball. Then every day I go to the gym and work towards it. My fight is what keeps me alive.

After my dad died, I didn't have it. I knew that I wanted to do *something*, but I didn't know what that thing was. And if a purpose hadn't come along soon I would have started looking for something, anything, to feel a high. When I got to Wellington and Kenny said I would need to be at training every morning, I figured that must be it. I went in full steam and used it as a distraction from thinking about Dad.

Pretty quickly I got addicted to the feeling of improving and that became my fight. The end goal has never been the NBA, because there *is* no end goal. I just want to keep getting better.

As long as I end each day knowing I'm better in some way than I was when I started it, I'm happy.

Having that mindset means I'll never be complacent with my game. I know I can expand my skillset because I've seen guys like Marc Gasol go from being exclusively a big man to now playing all over the court. When I train with MB, I'm still doing everything you'll see me do on court, plus just as much that you might not see for years.

At present I am doing well in my role and doing exactly what is asked of me. But the game is always getting quicker and evolving, and soon it won't be enough to just be a good big man. That's why I practice shooting from everywhere and shoot three-pointers every practice. That's why I have been working on Euro steps for months, but you've only seen one in a game. That's why I'm not afraid to defend on the perimeter, because I know one day my game will exist beyond it.

Every day I'm working to be better and every day I am better. You just might not see the results for a while because I have to make sure everything's perfect before I bring it into game situations. Trust me, I *will* drain a three by the time I retire.

The flip side to all of this is that if I wake up one day and don't have that fight to keep getting better, things will go downhill quickly. It sounds grim, but it's fairly simple—the only thing keeping me alive is that constant fight, no matter what it is. As soon as I stop chasing something, that means I've given up.

The good thing is that I know there are areas outside of basketball where I can direct my fight. When I was at school and needed the grades to keep going with basketball, I put my fight into that. It was a slog and I now have so much respect for all those creative people working their brains harder than I work my body. It's exhausting for me just to think about it. But it's also something I want to improve on, so I can see myself going back to school and putting my energy into learning, which I try to do every day anyway.

I would absolutely love to be in the league long enough to get dunked on by a fellow Kiwi at the beginning of his career. How awesome would that be? It's cool being the first New Zealander to do certain things in the NBA, but now that I've shown it's possible, it would be even cooler to see other kids take it further. We have the talent in New Zealand, there's no doubt about that, we just need the systems and pathways in place so that kids can stay on track and not lose out because they're poor or live in the wrong city.

I want to keep growing my camps and to start providing more specialized coaching to the young players who show great potential. I was given the right opportunities and breaks in my life that allowed me to reach heights many thought were unachievable. Now that I've gotten to a place of excellence and privilege, I want others to join me. If I have my way, New Zealand will be a basketball nation among the best in the world before I die. That's the kind of legacy I want to help build. I know my dad would be proud of that.

Ever since Dad passed away there have been occasions when I wish he could experience something with me—like the time I had to be taught how to shave by a friend's dad instead of my own. During big games I'll remember him and wonder what he would think about things. He was always such a straight shooter I'm sure he'd have some funny ideas about the NBA and fame. It's not that I want him to be proud of what I've achieved, I'd just like to have a chat with him about what I've been up to. Hear his thoughts on how I'm doing. He was always good for a yarn.

Without him here, I just play for me. I play hard and train hard so that when I'm all done I can look back and say I was my best. For now, there are games to be played and rings to be won. There's so much more that I can achieve, and so much more for everyone to see. So I'll keep fighting until they tell me to stop. Then I'll fight a little more.

GLOSSARY

AIR BALL—A shot that doesn't even hit the rim or backboard. Air balls are usually followed by a deep sense of shame.

ALLEY-OOP—When a player throws the ball towards the basket for their teammate, who catches the ball midair and scores, usually with a dunk. It's pretty cool.

AND-ONE—The **free throw** awarded to a shooter who is fouled while scoring.

ARC—The three-point line. Somewhere I generally try to avoid.

ASSIST—A pass to a teammate who scores a basket immediately or after one **dribble**.

BIG/BIG MAN—A man who is big and plays basketball.

BLOCK OUT/BOX OUT—Making sure your opponent doesn't get a rebound by pushing them away with your bum.

BOTS—Comes from the Samoan word "fiapoto," meaning someone who tries to be smart but fails.

BOUGIE—Trying to be fancy but failing.

CENTRE (U.S.: CENTER)—The biggest big man. A center's job is to control the area under the basket and get rebounds.

COURT—Lorde wrote a song about a tennis court. Now imagine basketball hoops at either end. That's pretty much a basketball court.

CUTTER—Someone who is cutting, which is running towards the hoop and looking for a pass. My job on defense is to bump the cutters when they pass by me because I guard the hoop and no one's allowed near it.

DOUBLE-DOUBLE—Gaining double-digit figures in two positive statistical categories (e.g., 12 points, 14 **rebounds**).

DRIBBLE—When saliva rolls down your chin. Also, bouncing the ball.

DUNK—You don't know what a dunk is? Just ask anyone on the street and they'll demonstrate with whatever they're holding and a rubbish bin.

FADEAWAY—A fadeaway is a shot taken while jumping backwards, away from the basket, but still facing it. YouTube "Dirk Nowitzki fadeaway" to see the greatest fadeaway in history.

FAST BREAK—A quick basket scored through swift ball movement down the court after a defensive **rebound** and before the other team has set up their defense.

FLOATER—A shot with a high arc. If the ball looks like it's gone abnormally high on its way to the net, it's a good floater.

FORWARD—One of the three standard player positions, forwards are mainly responsible for scoring and **rebounding**. *See* **power forward** and **small forward**.

FOUL—There are so many ways to foul someone in basketball, both on offense and on defense. Some contact is illegal and a foul while other contact is legal and fine. It's impossible to explain but if you get called for a foul, that's bad.

FOUL OUT—The personal limit in the NBA is six fouls. Foul six times and you're out for the rest of the game.

FOUR MAN—Someone who is strong enough to play in the post if needed but is versatile enough to act as a **guard**, too. A four man can do everything.

FREE THROW—A free shot given to a player when they're fouled while shooting. For **technical fouls** one free throw is awarded and for flagrant fouls you get two.

GUARD—The smaller guys in a team who start the plays out by the three-point line and shoot more three-pointers.

HOOK SHOT—Classic shot used by most big men, because the shot is released sideways with a nearly fully extended arm, which makes it hard to block.

HOPS—Having a good vertical jump. If you can't jump, you don't have *bad* hops, you have *no* hops.

HORI—Being a bit rugged. You can't just call anyone hori though, you're only allowed to say it about people you actually like, and who like you. Some people say it disrespectfully, I just say it to my brothers.

IN THE BONUS—When you've fouled too many times and now your opponent gets "bonus" **free throws** for every new **foul**.

INBOUND (pass)—Passing the ball IN from out-of-BOUNDS, hence INBOUND.

JUMP SHOT—Surely you figured this out by looking at the words "jump" and "shot"?

KEY—The painted circle and lines by the hoop that, funnily enough, look a little like a keyhole.

LAYUP—The simplest way to score points and yet the hardest to explain. It's when a player dribbles towards the hoop and scores a basket while still in motion, usually in **fast breaks**. Seriously, it's really hard to explain.

LOW-POST AREA—The area closest to the basket.

PAINT—The **key**.

PERIMETER—Has a few different meanings but most people know it as the three-point line.

PICK-AND-ROLL—Setting a **screen** (pick) then turning (rolling) to block the defender more while you cut to the basket for a pass.

POINT GUARD—Usually the shortest player on the court. Runs the plays and argues with the refs a lot.

POST—The area on court closest to the basket.

POST UP—Setting up with your back to the hoop.

POSTERIZE—Dunking on someone so bad a photo of it could be used on a poster.

POWER FORWARD—A big guy who's not as tall as a center.

PUTBACK—When you "put" the ball "back" into the hoop after **rebounding**.

REBOUND/REBOUNDING—Gaining possession after the ball—wait for it—*rebounds* off the basket.

ROOKIE—In the NBA, a player in their first season. In life, someone who's just done something dumb.

SCREEN/SET A SCREEN—Establish a stationary position to act as a block for your teammate to use to get rid of their defender. If you're a guy, cover your nuts when setting a screen because someone will probably be running right into you.

SEAL—To establish a good position by "sealing" your defender and keeping them behind you.

SMALL BALL/SMALL GAME—A style of play that favors use of smaller players for their speed, agility, and increased scoring (often from the three-point line).

SMALL FORWARD—Smaller than a **forward**, bigger than a **guard**.

TECHNICAL FOUL—A foul for unsportsmanlike non-contact behavior, which is usually complaining to a ref or taunting your opponent.

TIP-OFF—The start of the game.

TRANSITION—The short time after the defending team gets a **rebound** but before a play is set up. Good transition means quick ball movement down the court and **fast break layups**.

TRAVEL—When you take too many steps without **dribbling**, you get called for a travel then run back down the court and think very hard about what you just did.

TRIPLE-DOUBLE—Double-digit figures in three positive statistical categories (e.g. 12 points, 14 **rebounds**, 10 **assists**).

CO-AUTHOR'S NOTE

I first met Steven, predictably, at a basketball training held by Kenny McFadden early in 2009. Steven was a center and I was a point guard, yet he outperformed me in all the ball-handling drills. Over the next five years I watched as Steven went from strength to strength and the world was able to see the brilliance I'd seen in that cold Wellington gym so many times.

When Steven found out I was a writer in 2016, he asked me if I'd ever written a book. I answered no, but that I thought I could. And that was enough for him. We were suddenly co-authors and I was given a front-row seat to his current life and to his memories. Thank you to Steven and the team at Penguin Random House for allowing me to help tell this incredible story. Thank you to all of Steven's family and friends who donated their memories and thoughts to this project, it wouldn't have worked without you. Thank you to Samuel Marsden Collegiate for giving me a space to write. Thank you to Top House and Bottom House for the laughter at home. And thank you to all the Guilty Denvers at The Spinoff for the laughter at work. A special thank you to Toby Manhire for making every chapter better.

To my siblings—Edwin, Jerome, Rosemarie, Victoria, Leone, Bernard, Christel, Kenneth, and Temara—thank you for always providing plenty of writing fodder and harsh critiques of my jokes. To my dad, thank you for encouraging my love of sport, particularly basketball. And to my mum the biggest thanks, for being the greatest fighter I know. This one's for you.

Madeleine Chapman
May 2018